THE QUEEN'S PICTURES

OLD MASTERS FROM
THE ROYAL COLLECTION

THE QUEEN'S PICTURES

OLD MASTERS FROM THE ROYAL COLLECTION

Christopher Lloyd

SURVEYOR OF
THE QUEEN'S PICTURES

Royal Collection Enterprises Limited

British Library Cataloguing in Publication Data
A CIP catalogue record for this book is available from the
British Library.

ISBN: 297 83276 x

This catalogue was produced by
Weidenfeld and Nicolson Ltd for
Royal Collection Enterprises Ltd

Editor: Lucas Dietrich
Designed by Harry Green

Typeset by Keyspools Ltd, Newton le Willows, Lancs.
Printed and bound in Italy

CONTENTS

FOREWORD
HRH The Prince of Wales
PAGE 7

SPONSOR'S FOREWORD
PAGE 9

PREFACE BY DIRECTORS
PAGE 10

ACKNOWLEDGEMENTS
PAGE 12

INTRODUCTION
PAGE 14

THE CATALOGUE
PAGE 33

GENEALOGICAL TREE
OF ROYAL COLLECTORS
PAGE 94

FURTHER READING
PAGE 95

INDEX
PAGE 96

FOREWORD

HRH The Prince of Wales

This is the first time that a group of important paintings from the Royal Collection has been shown outside the United Kingdom. I am particularly pleased that the three countries where the pictures will be shown – New Zealand, Australia and Canada – have such close historical associations with Britain, and that the pictures will be made accessible to the widest possible cross-section of people – including in two of the newest museum buildings in the world.

The selection of thirty major paintings has been specially devised for this exhibition. It demonstrates the broad range of the Royal Collection as well as the changing taste of royal collectors through the centuries. Works by Italian, Flemish, Dutch, French and British artists from the sixteenth to the nineteenth centuries are included. Many of the paintings are interesting not only as works of art but because of their historical associations. Rembrandt's *The Shipbuilder and his Wife*, Cuyp's *An Evening Landscape* and *Soldiers of the Tenth Light Dragoons* by Stubbs are outright masterpieces. There are outstanding portraits by Van Dyck, Hals, Hogarth and Lawrence. The pictures by Artemisia Gentileschi (*Self-Portrait*), Allori (*Judith*), Agasse (*The Nubian Giraffe*), Winterhalter (*The First of May*) and Lady Butler (*The Roll Call*) are fascinating both for their subject-matter and for the circumstances in which they were painted.

The wide range of the Royal Collection reflects the personal interests and tastes of individual monarchs. Until now, these paintings have always been hung in Royal Palaces, where they were seen and enjoyed by a relatively limited audience. In recent months, however, the Royal Collection has changed its status. From 1 April 1993 it was established as a trust administered by a board of trustees. One of its main objectives is to make the collection more accessible to an ever-increasing public interested in the visual arts. An important means to do this is to arrange for exhibitions to travel overseas, in addition to the usual displays put on in The Queen's Gallery at Buckingham Palace. I hope that all who see the paintings in this exhibition for the first time will derive real pleasure from them.

SPONSOR'S FOREWORD

American Express Company is extremely proud to be sponsoring *The Queen's Pictures: Old Masters from the Royal Collection*.

We consider it an honour to be part of such a distinguished undertaking: for not only is this the largest number of paintings from this magnificent collection to be sent abroad as a single exhibition, but the thirty paintings represented here are outstanding works of art acquired by British monarchs over three hundred years and include masterpieces by Rembrandt, Van Dyck, Hogarth, Hals and Gainsborough, among others. It is precisely because these works deserve to be seen by the broadest possible audience that they are travelling, by means of this landmark exhibition, from the Royal residences of Great Britain to the National Galleries of New Zealand, Australia and Canada.

The American Express Foundation has long lent support, through the American Express Philanthropic Program, to international cultural projects of special merit in view of American Express Company's global presence in travel and tourism. We hope you will join us in expressing gratitude to Her Majesty The Queen for her generosity in making this extraordinary exhibition possible.

R. CRAIG HOENSHELL
President, International

AMERICAN EXPRESS TRAVEL RELATED SERVICES COMPANY, INC.

PREFACE BY DIRECTORS

The world is seeing major shifts in social, political and cultural terms as we move towards the end of the twentieth century. In cultural terms these shifts have involved addressing questions of national identity and the developing relationships between diverse peoples. In all this change, the world's cultural heritage provides us with both an anchor and a point of departure for a positive global future. Against this background, wonderful exhibitions like *The Queen's Pictures: Old Masters from the Royal Collection* become doubly significant and enriching.

In the context of this country's emerging consciousness of its bicultural foundation, a sampling of the richness of the Royal Collection provides an opportunity for all who visit to grow in their understanding of the European heritage of the forebears of what we now often refer to as the pakeha or tangata Tiriti, the people of the Treaty, in Aotearoa New Zealand.

We are grateful to Her Majesty Queen Elizabeth for making available such a range of quality work to audiences in the capital cities of New Zealand, Australia and Canada. The thirty paintings in this exhibition span three centuries of the high points of Europe's artistic endeavour. Not all of these works are normally on public display. The Museum of New Zealand Te Papa Tongarewa proudly joins with our colleagues at the National Gallery of Australia and the National Gallery of Canada and our respective sponsors in presenting *The Queen's Pictures: Old Masters from the Royal Collection.*

JENNY HARPER
Director Museum Projects

CHERYLL SOTHERAN
Chief Executive
MUSEUM OF NEW ZEALAND TE PAPA TONGAREWA

The National Gallery of Australia is proud and honoured to host *The Queen's Pictures: Old Masters from the Royal Collection.* The thirty paintings that form the exhibition have been carefully selected from royal residences to provide a small but singular collection of masterpieces of European paintings from the sixteenth to the nineteenth century. These works are outstanding examples in their own right and form a superb representative exhibition of the rarely seen European paintings from the Royal Collection.

Her Majesty The Queen has offered this exhibition to the National Galleries of New Zealand, Australia and Canada, and for this we are deeply

indebted. I join my fellow Australians in thanking Her Majesty for this unique opportunity.

In the period of dynamic change, as Australia's population grows and cultural horizons widen, it is important not to lose sight of the European heritage that underpins our society.

The exhibition has been assembled not only for its art-historical and cultural significance but for the immense enjoyment it will undoubtably bring to Australian audiences.

BETTY CHURCHER
Director
NATIONAL GALLERY OF AUSTRALIA

The exhibition of *The Queen's Pictures: Old Masters from the Royal Collection* is an occasion for celebration and gratitude. These thirty pictures will bring joy to their many viewers, not only because they are the work of great artists through the centuries but because this is a unique opportunity to see these works together as a group – some of which are not always on public view – and to contemplate them at our leisure.

Canada's National Gallery shares this wonderful exhibition with the National Galleries of New Zealand and Australia. We rejoice in a heritage that, with all the diverse cultures that make our nations thrive today, brings us together in a commonwealth of shared ideals and values.

As our world becomes ever more complex, great works of art serve to remind us of the creative genius, wherever those works were produced. *The Queen's Pictures: Old Masters from the Royal Collection* shows us examples of European art at its zenith, and for this the National Gallery of Canada and its public are deeply grateful.

It is a privilege and an honour to receive *The Queen's Pictures: Old Masters from the Royal Collection* at the National Gallery of Canada. I know our visitors will join me in expressing their gratitude to Her Majesty The Queen for her generosity in lending these masterworks to us.

Dr Shirley L. Thomson
Director
NATIONAL GALLERY OF CANADA

ACKNOWLEDGEMENTS

An exhibition that travels to New Zealand, Australia and Canada and involves such great distances requires careful organization. I am delighted that paintings from the Royal Collection will be shown in these countries, and I am grateful to Sir Hamish Hay, Chairman of the Board of the Museum of New Zealand Te Papa Tongarewa; The Hon. Lionel Bowen, Chairman of the Council of the National Gallery of Australia; and Mr Jean-Claude Delorme, Chairman of the Board of Trustees from the National Gallery of Canada for supporting the project. It has been a singular pleasure to work with the three directors of these institutions – Ms Jenny Harper, Betty Churcher, Dr Shirley Thomson – who were full of encouragement and enthusiasm from the start. That the exhibition can take place at all is due to the generosity and help of our sponsors – American Express Company – who so readily and sympathetically appreciated that the main purpose of the exhibition is to display outstanding paintings to the broadest possible audience.

A large number of people have helped with the preparations of the exhibition. Thanks are due to the conservators of the Royal Collection – Viola Pemberton-Pigott, Karen Ashworth, Rosanna Eadie, Cliona Bacon and Elizabeth Calvert – for preparing the paintings and frames for travel. The relining of *The Shipbuilder and his Wife* by Rembrandt (No. 9) and *An Evening Landscape* by Aelbert Cuyp (No. 14) was undertaken by Simon Bobak and carried out with great care and skill. Temporary frames for *The Adoration of the Shepherds* by Jacopo Bassano (No. 1) and the *Portrait of Sir Walter Scott* by Sir Thomas Lawrence (No. 27) were supplied by Arnold Wiggins & Son Ltd. Additional thanks are due to the transport agents, Kevin Richardson of Momart Ltd, who ensured the safe transit of the works; David Moffat, of Bain Clarkson Ltd, for advising on insurance; David Fellowes and John Roffey of Kent Services Ltd for providing the travelling cases. The Hon. James Stourton of Sotheby's deserves special thanks for valuing the pictures.

I am especially grateful to the restorers at the borrowing institutions in New Zealand, Merv Hutchinson and Lesley Cobb; Australia, Trevor Hoyne and Bronwyn Ormsby; and Canada, Marion Barclay, for monitoring and safeguarding the condition of the pictures on their long journey across the world and while they were on exhibition at the three national galleries. A key aspect of this exhibition has been the opportunity it has provided for cooperation between the Royal Collection and the staff of the Museum of New Zealand Te Papa Tongarewa, the National Gallery of Australia and the National Gallery of Canada: this has been a very successful strategy in the area of restoration.

The same high standards have also been applied to the administrative aspects of the project. From the outset The Hon. Cazzy Neville (Exhibitions Assistant to the Surveyor) acted on behalf of the Royal Collection as co-ordinator, dealing with such matters as the selection list, design and layout of the exhibition, government indemnity and insurance, transportation and couriers, as well as assisting with the catalogue, supporting literature and publicity. Her contribution has been invaluable, but she has in turn benefited from the experience of working with Sally Cantwell, Hubert Klaassens, Fritha Marriage and Craig Pollock (Museum of New Zealand Te Papa Tongarewa); Alan Dodge, Alan Froud, Kevin Munn and Warwick Reeder (National Gallery of Australia); and Delphine Bishop, Kate Laing, Catherine Johnston and Karen Lisa Oxorn (National Gallery of Canada). Other members of the Royal Collection have also enjoyed working with their counterparts in their respective fields of expertise:

Edward Hewlett (Managing Director, Royal Collection Enterprises Ltd), Dickie Arbiter (Director of Media Affairs) and Stephen Spencer (Retail Manager, Royal Collection Enterprises Ltd).

I am particularly grateful to Weidenfeld and Nicolson for publishing the catalogue. Michael Dover oversaw the publication and liaised with the designer, Harry Green, and editor, Lucas Dietrich, both of whose contributions have been of the greatest significance in producing such an elegant catalogue. Emma Scrase and Susannah Morris prepared the typescript.

A great deal of the excitement in organizing this exhibition has been derived from the fact that it is a joint venture, and correspondingly it is hoped that the pleasure gained from seeing this group of paintings belonging to the Royal Collection will be spread far and wide.

INTRODUCTION

The paintings in the Royal Collection can be approached in a number of ways. First and foremost, they comprise a distinguished collection of pictures that dates back as far as the late fifteenth century with the establishment of the Tudor dynasty, and over four centuries some seven thousand paintings have been amassed. Although all the monarchs have added pictures to the collection in accordance with their individual taste or needs, only a few have been recognized as genuine collectors. These are Charles I (1625–49), George IV (1820–1830) and Queen Victoria (1837–1901), and to a certain extent it is true to say that many of the greatest works in the collection were acquired as a result of their efforts. George III (1760–1820) cannot technically be described as a collector of paintings, since his chief interest lay in books, scientific instruments and clocks. Yet an important purchase in 1762 and his patronage of a wide variety of artists are important elements in the development of the collection.

Certain other royal figures should not be overlooked: Henry, Prince of Wales (1594–1612), the elder brother of Charles I; Frederick, Prince of Wales (1707–51), the father of George III; and Prince Albert (1819–61), whom Queen Victoria married in 1840, were notable connoisseurs. The groups of paintings they have all contributed make the Royal Collection today one of the finest holdings in existence. Furthermore, while the collection can be considered essentially private, by virtue of the manner in which it was assembled, it has in recent years moved more into the public sphere.

A second line of approach to the Royal Collection lies in its association with the institution of monarchy. Certainly up until the present century all monarchs relied upon portraiture as the principal means of establishing their identity and status. Thus the evolution of certain categories of British painting, such as state portraits, royal conversation pieces and portraits of royal children, can for the most part be traced by direct reference to the Royal Collection. Although these categories are, in turn, related to the mainstream of art, it should not be forgotten that court art in earlier centuries was on its own account deeply influential. Some artists succeeded at court while others failed, but whatever the results, their work was always carefully scrutinized by a wider public. Painting in the royal context was also expected to provide a record of fact. Events of historical significance, extending from the time of Henry VIII to the end of Queen Victoria's long reign, were often committed to canvas simply as a visual record. These events included ceremonial or diplomatic occasions, marriages and births, as well as military scenes. Such compositions form part of the wider evolution of historical painting in Britain. Similarly, the numerous depictions of horses and dogs in the Royal Collection illustrate not only monarchy's long affiliation with field sports but the development of sporting pictures during the eighteenth and nineteenth centuries.

Third, the Royal Collection can be considered with reference to the buildings in which the paintings are displayed, since so many of the paintings have historical links with specific residences. Today the pictures are concentrated in Buckingham Palace, Windsor Castle, Kensington Palace, St James's Palace, Kew Palace, Osborne House, Sandringham House, the Palace of Holyroodhouse, Frogmore House and Balmoral Castle. Each residence has varied in significance from dynasty to dynasty and even from monarch to monarch, but several – most importantly Whitehall Palace, which was burnt in 1698 – have not survived into the twentieth century. The extensive documentation on the Royal Collection, however, means that the arrangement of the pictures in many of the remaining, and in the lost, residences can be reconstructed almost on a room-to-room basis. The primary sources for this information are the inventories dating from the sixteenth century that list the paintings in the various buildings over the centuries. They can be supplemented by schematic representations of picture hangs, watercolours of interiors and, ultimately, photographs. Study of these inventories and related visual material reveals changes in taste and adds an extra dimension to an appreciation of the Royal Collection. A more detailed discussion of each of these approaches forms the basis of this introduction, which is accordingly divided into three sections: Princes, Pictures and Palaces.

It is apparent, therefore, that the historical context is as significant as the art-historical elements in the Royal Collection. As the largest private collection in the world, it is a unique survival. Whereas royal collections in such countries as France, Germany, Spain, Austria, Holland, Russia and Scandinavia have been ceded to the state as a result of political changes and now form the nucleus of national collections, the British Royal Collection has been retained by the crown. The beheading of Charles I in 1649 led to the disastrous dispersal of the collection in a series of sales. Only a small amount was recovered at the Restoration in 1660, so the collection had to be gradually replenished. Because it is hung within those buildings with which it has long been associated, the collection is not, strictly speaking, comparable with a museum. The paintings, like the sculpture, furniture and porcelain, form an integral part of the overall decoration of royal residences. Often shown according to historical precedent, in some areas they even serve a specific iconographical purpose. This, combined with the exercising of personal taste, indicates that the Royal Collection does not share the same aims as a museum. The paintings do not, for instance, provide a comprehensive survey of the history of Western art. There are pictures of superlative quality, but there are also some gaps (no canvases by Poussin, Watteau, Goya, Turner or Constable, and no major examples of Pre-Raphaelite or Impressionist painting, let alone modern art), which in a major museum today would probably prove to be embarrassing. To criticize the Royal Collection for what might appear to be *lapsi calami* is to misunderstand its historical significance and to overlook its traditional function.

PRINCES

Charles I (Fig. 1) was born with an acquisitive instinct, and it was he who formed the finest collection of paintings ever assembled in Britain. He

FIG. 1 Sir Anthony Van Dyck (1599–1641) *Charles I.* Oil on canvas, 1636.

acquired altogether some 1,500 pictures, including several masterpieces by artists of the calibre of Raphael, Leonardo da Vinci, Titian, Veronese, Caravaggio and Correggio. What is most surprising is the speed with which the paintings were accumulated, since Charles I only collected in earnest for about twenty years, but the breaking up of the Royal Collection was equally dramatic, following the King's execution in January 1649. His collection was important because it rivalled the cultural achievements of Italian, French, Hapsburg and Spanish rulers. As such, Charles I established for himself a reputation as a major patron of the arts in Europe. Also, by introducing so many important works of art into the country and by employing leading artists like Rubens and Van Dyck, he influenced the development of British art. His collection, in effect, acted as a catalyst, and its cosmopolitan nature released British art from its insularity.

Charles I inherited a love of art from his father, James I (James VI of Scotland), who was an intellectual. Albeit not a very pleasant individual, he conducted a clever foreign policy and was especially learned in political theory. It was said of James I that 'he loved beasts better than men' (referring to his love of hunting), but of his wife, Anne of Denmark, it was said that she preferred pictures to the company of living people. She is reported to have gone into her gallery at Oatlands Palace specifically to look at her pictures on the day before her death. There, she would have enjoyed a number of religious pictures (she was a convert to Catholicism), numerous portraits and some mythological and topographical pictures, as well as still lifes.

The eldest son of James I and Anne of Denmark was Henry, Prince of Wales (No. 3), who personified the Renaissance – somewhat belatedly – in England. A lover of literature and the arts, he was also a warrior prince who took a particular interest in arms, armour, tournaments and ships. For many years he was the chief patron of Inigo Jones, but he also made contact with French and Italian artists and craftsmen. It is difficult to reconstruct the complete collection of paintings gathered by Henry, Prince of Wales, even though the royal cypher (*HP*) was applied on the backs of his pictures. It seems that, although he often had his own portrait painted, his collection was not overstocked with portraits. Instead, there was a preponderance of religious paintings, marine pictures, classical subjects and battle pieces – all of which reflected both personal interests and artistic developments in Europe. Henry, Prince of Wales, died in 1612 at only eighteen years of age, leaving his younger brother as heir to the throne.

Charles I was created Prince of Wales in 1616 and became King in 1625. Even before that his interest in art had manifested itself. A key episode in the formation of his taste was the visit made in 1623 with George Villiers, first Duke of Buckingham, to Spain in order to find a bride. It was on this occasion that Charles I saw the Spanish royal collection over which the young Philip IV (himself only eighteen years old) presided. The collection was rich in Flemish paintings by such masters as Hieronymus Bosch and the Brueghel family, but the greatest glory was the wide range of works by Titian commissioned by Philip IV's grandfather, Philip II. Charles I was given two famous paintings by Titian (*Portrait of Charles V with a Hound* and the *Venus del Pardo*) and was offered yet other prestigious works by the artist. These last were withheld, however, when the marriage negotiations broke down, but it would not be surprising if Charles I returned to London, resolved to form a collection to rival that of Philip IV. Significantly, two years later Rubens described Charles I as 'the greatest amateur of painting among the princes of the world'.

The city of London had itself by this time become an important locus for collectors of whose interests Charles I would no doubt have been aware. The Duke of Buckingham, for example, had a meteoric rise to power as a favourite of James I, but he suffered a tragic death in 1628 at the hands of an assassin. Politically speaking, Buckingham was a parvenu, and he used art as a way of bolstering his social position. For him to possess works of art was to hold power and prestige, and it was a way of exercising influence. His collection included major works by leading Venetian artists of the High Renaissance but also examples by contemporary artists, such as Guido Reni and Rubens. Following the assassination of the Duke of Buckingham, the collection owned by the third Marquess (later first Duke) of Hamilton assumed great importance. Hamilton was a greedy, ambitious and vain Scottish nobleman, but his collection of six hundred paintings (in part inherited from his father) contained masterpieces by Antonello da Messina, Giorgione and Titian. Though distinguished, the collection was to some extent based on opportunism.

By contrast, Thomas Howard, second Earl of Arundel, was a real connoisseur who travelled extensively in Europe with his wife, Alathea, and displayed powers of artistic discernment as a collector that placed him far above Buckingham or Hamilton. His interests extended beyond paintings to embrace drawings, prints, books and particularly antique art. As a man, he was taciturn, moody, withdrawn, but he befriended artists like Inigo Jones, Wenceslaus Hollar, Rubens and Van Dyck. Like his contemporaries, Arundel greatly admired Venetian painting, but he also had a penchant for Northern European art, especially the works of Hans Holbein the Younger and Dürer.

There was, therefore, a large concentration of art established in the centre of London by the 1620s and 1630s. Rubens remarked in 1629, 'I must admit that when it comes to the pictures by the hands of first-class masters, I have never seen such a large number in one place as in the royal palaces in England and in the gallery of the late Duke of Buckingham'. This certainly provides a context for Charles I's collection, but it also amounts to a close network of contacts. His collection was in fact much enlarged by a series of exchanges with fellow collectors. It was in this way, for instance, that he obtained *St George and the Dragon* by Raphael (now in Washington D.C., National Gallery of Art) and *St John the Baptist* by Leonardo da Vinci (Paris, Musée du Louvre) in exchange for works by northern masters.

The King's preference, however, was always for the more seductive charms of the Venetian school. He also received gifts from foreign powers, as well as from private individuals, all proffered for a variety of motives. Yet the King remained acquisitive in his own right, employing numerous agents, negotiators and special envoys to locate works of art. Indeed, it was through an agent that Charles I made the most spectacular purchase of his reign: the Gonzaga collection in Mantua. The declining fortunes of the Gonzaga family forced them in 1628–9 to sell their outstanding collection – one of the finest in Italy. Against considerable opposition Charles I acquired numerous paintings by Mantegna, Titian, Giulio Romano, Correggio, Caravaggio, Annibale Carracci and Domenico Fetti. The character of his collection was transformed by this dramatic purchase and the King was now on equal terms with his European rivals.

Charles I was keen to repeat this coup, but the changing political scene and shortage of money prevented him from making similarly dramatic purchases. Parallel to these acquisitions, however, was Charles I's patronage of contemporary painters. His attempts to woo leading Italian painters proved difficult, partly owing to the terrible climate in Britain and partly for religious reasons, but, on the other hand, Rubens and Van Dyck were both enticed by the prospect of work at the English court. The paintings that Van Dyck carried out in London between 1632 and his death on the eve of the Civil War in 1641 transformed painting in England and remained influential well into the eighteenth century. Van Dyck (No. 10) brought not only technical skill to portraiture but the psychological insight evident in the gestures, poise, deportment and characterization of his sitters. Here was a painter working in England over a long period who could stand comparison with Titian, Rubens and Velásquez. One painting in particular by Van Dyck reveals a great deal about the court of Charles I. *Cupid and Psyche* is Titianesque in treatment, and it is the only mythological picture to have survived from this stage of Van Dyck's career. The subject no doubt appealed to a court that had become divorced from reality and was prepared to seek solace in Neo-Platonic ideals.

Van Dyck's portraits of the King display all Charles I's characteristics: his elegance, refinement, intelligence, dignity and shyness, as well as his single-mindedness, obtuseness and stubborness combined with surprising physical strength and mental resilience. Historians will continue to argue about the degree to which the King's love of art weakened his political position. The attention paid to art may indeed have helped to alienate the country, as the court became increasingly introverted, thereby leading to a serious misjudgment of the mounting political and financial pressures.

The sale of Charles I's collection by the government of Oliver Cromwell after the execution of the King in 1649 was a cultural calamity. The works were first valued (the most expensive was the *Madonna della Perla* by Raphael at £2,000, while the *Portrait of the Artist's Mother* by Rembrandt was valued at only £4) and then sold to pay off the King's debts. Most of the creditors were artisans. Many buyers formed syndicates to acquire whole groups of works that were then sold on, but the chief beneficiaries were French collectors such as Cardinal Mazarin and Philip IV of Spain. The sales gave a tremendous impetus to the creation of an art market. Ironically, many of those paintings acquired by Charles I's rivals were eventually yielded up and can now be found on the walls of the greatest galleries in the world – in Berlin, Paris, Amsterdam, Vienna, Madrid, New York and Washington D. C. The only works retained by Oliver Cromwell during the Protectorate were *The Triumphs of Caesar* by Mantegna (now at Hampton Court Palace) and the Raphael Cartoons (now on loan to the Victoria and Albert Museum), which were presumably deemed to be appropriate. The Raphael Cartoons had been acquired in Genoa in 1623 for use by the Mortlake tapestry factory founded by James I, and the *Triumphs of Caesar* had formed part of the Gonzaga collection.

Only one other royal collector of paintings can

FIG. 2 Sir Thomas Lawrence (1769–1830), *George IV*. Oil on canvas, 1821.

compare with Charles I: George IV (Fig. 2). There are, in fact, several parallels to be drawn between Charles I and George IV as collectors. Both were influenced at the outset by members of their families. George IV's grandfather, Frederick, Prince of Wales, had been a discerning collector conscious of the achievements of Charles I and keen to emulate him. As though in recognition of these predecessors, the antiquarian scholar, George Vertue, who held long discussions on painting with Frederick, Prince of Wales, remarked, 'no Prince since King Charles the First took so much pleasure nor observations on works of art or artists'. Frederick added some distinguished pictures by Rubens and Van Dyck to the collection and took an interest in the work of Jan

Brueghel the Elder and David Teniers the Younger, thus extending the collection's representation of Flemish painting. He also sought out works by seventeenth-century Dutch (No. 6), French (No. 12), Spanish and Italian painters, as well as being an avid patron of such British artists as John Wootton (No. 18). His portrait was painted by artists as diverse as Jean-Baptiste Van Loo, Thomas Hudson, Joseph Highmore, Philippe Mercier and Jacopo Amigoni, which reflects the range of his taste. Above all, Frederick, Prince of Wales, had an undeniable enthusiasm for art. The maiden voyage early in June 1732 of his State Barge designed by William Kent (now in the National Maritime Museum) was the occasion for a visit to Somerset House to view pictures from the collection being restored. He was accompanied by members of his family and 'a Set of Musick'.

George IV's father and mother were also influential in the formation of his taste. While George III pondered his books, tinkered with his clocks, calibrated his scientific instruments and enjoyed his farming, Queen Charlotte interested herself chiefly in botany, porcelain and jewellery. Even though George III and Queen Charlotte lived abstemiously, it seems likely that the ambience they created at Buckingham House and Windsor Castle kindled the consuming interest their son had in the arts. The painting *Queen Charlotte at her Dressing Table* by Johann Zoffany (Fig. 3) dating from *c.*1765 epitomizes the taste of George IV's parents and anticipates his own. Painted with a remarkable degree of

FIG. 3 Johann Zoffany (1733/4–1810), *Queen Charlotte at her Dressing Table*. Oil on canvas, *c.* 1765.

exactitude, Zoffany's depiction faithfully records the interior, which includes a long-case clock, chinoiserie figures and a carpet in the Persian style. The picture is particularly informative not only about the furnishings but about the elegant contents of the dressing table. There are also glimpses of the paintings newly acquired from Consul Joseph Smith in Venice, but in the midst of this scene is the diminutive figure of the young George IV dressed as a soldier in a Telemachus uniform (the helmet is decorated with a tiny set of Prince of Wales's feathers). The painting could almost literally be a dress rehearsal for his adult life.

At the annual dinner of the Royal Academy in 1811 George IV gave a speech in which he said, 'Others might be more able to judge of the excellence of works of art [but they] could not exceed him in his love of the arts or in [his] wishes for their prosperity'. As with Charles I, he was fortunate in the time at which he was collecting. The upheaval caused by the French Revolution and the Napoleonic wars in Spain, Italy, Russia and the Netherlands resulted in the art market being flooded with paintings. The famous collection – the finest in Europe – belonging to Joseph, Duc d'Orléans, was sold in 1792 and portions of it acquired by a syndicate of British noblemen. Such was the flood of masterpieces that industrialists, merchants and financiers, in addition to aristocrats, created significant collections. The concentration of paintings in London rivalled that during the reign of Charles I, and the city was frequently visited by leading European connoisseurs. Supplying these collectors was a whole network of dealers, agents and middlemen keen to develop this expanding market.

George IV lived in a style that ran directly contrary to his father's principals. Carlton House in London and the Royal Pavilion in Brighton were the outstanding expressions of his extravagant and ornate taste. Carlton House was pulled down in 1827, and George IV then turned his attention to the redecoration of Buckingham House and Windsor Castle. As a collector he spent prodigiously. It was the scale and regularity of his spending that made him *primus inter pares* among the great collectors of his day. Regardless of mounting debts, he continued to spend money on building and works of art. Parliament became increasingly alarmed. Yet the impact of this incessant outlay is still apparent in the Picture Gallery in Buckingham Palace and the Grand Corridor in Windsor Castle. Although George IV personally oversaw the expansion of the Royal Collection, he did rely on advisers such as Lord Yarmouth (later the third Marquess of Hertford), Sir Charles Long (later Lord Farnborough), Walsh Porter and Sir Thomas Lawrence – all important connoisseurs and collectors in their own right.

As a collector of paintings George IV was essentially conservative. The thrust of his buying lay in seventeenth-century Dutch and Flemish schools, so the Royal Collection was augmented with works by Van Dyck, Rembrandt (No. 9), Cuyp (No. 14), Hobbema, Van de Velde, Ruisdael, Steen (No. 16), De Hooch (No. 15), Terborch, Ostade, Dou, Rubens and Teniers. Quality was the hallmark of George IV's purchases, both as regards artistic technique and provenance. The prices paid were usually high and the preference was for closely finished, precisely painted cabinet pictures. Like Charles I, George IV indulged in exchanges to obtain works that he particularly wanted, such as *Landscape with St George* by Rubens and *Christ and the Magdalen at the Tomb* by Rembrandt. In 1814, on buying the collection of Dutch pictures formed by the banker Sir Francis Baring – one of his more spectacular purchases – George IV discarded certain items, like the still lifes, that he did not wish to retain and sent them for sale with other pictures at Christie's.

Also in accordance with the taste of his day and as a passionate Francophile, George IV acquired French paintings (Nos. 8 and 22), although fewer than those of the Dutch and Flemish schools. In addition, he did a great deal to support British artists. Works by Reynolds, Gainsborough (No. 23), Stubbs (No. 26), Hoppner, Beechey, Lawrence (No. 27) are represented in the Royal

Collection in considerable numbers as a result of this enthusiasm, but George IV also took an interest in narrative painting, exemplified by such artists as Wilkie, Haydon and Mulready. The representation of paintings by Wilkie is especially instructive, since it incorporates both genre and historical subject matter. George IV's greatest act of patronage of British art was to commission from J. M. W. Turner a painting of *The Battle of Trafalgar* (1823–4) to form a pair with *The Glorious First of June* by P. J. de Loutherbourg in the Ante-Room of St James's Palace. *The Battle of Trafalgar* was the largest canvas Turner ever painted, but courtiers in the manner of self-appointed art critics found fault in the composition, decrying its nautical inaccuracies and impugning the artist's integrity. In the end George IV felt obliged to give both pictures away to Greenwich, where they hang today in the National Maritime Museum. This act of generosity upset the artist, and the gap in the Royal Collection has never been filled.

Certainly Queen Victoria made no attempt to rectify this situation, since according to George V, George IV's niece declared that Turner was mad. However, as Sir Oliver Millar has pointed out about Queen Victoria and Prince Albert, 'Theirs is the last moderately heroic chapter in the history of royal patronage and taste in this country'. Queen Victoria's collecting was worthy and dutiful; it was hardly ever inspired. She was frightened of spending money (unlike her uncle, George IV) and had a proclivity for second-rate artists. Her choice of painters veered towards the safe rather than the adventurous, and anything new or challenging was dismissed. As a result, many opportunities were lost. No major painting by a Pre-Raphaelite artist was added to the collection, and with respect to French painting, Queen Victoria clearly preferred the Salon to the Impressionists.

Despite these limitations, art did play an important role in Queen Victoria's life, and she was a frequent visitor to exhibitions. Fundamentally, painting was a means of recording her family, her interests and her country's achievements. No doubt her choice of artists 'was dictated by her own personal satisfaction. For a monarch who was so conscious of her public duty, the paintings she acquired were overwhelmingly private in their significance. In terms of numbers alone, portraits – including members of Queen Victoria's extended family so frequently gathered together for special occasions or anniversaries – predominate. Beyond these are portraits of those who worked for the Queen, of those whom she admired in public life, and even of her pets. All were diligently, sometimes skilfully, but rarely imaginatively, recorded for posterity in paint. British painters, like Wilkie, Hayter, Grant, Leslie and Lucas, failed to maintain the standards expected by the Queen, and she came to rely more and more on foreign artists, such as F. X. Winterhalter (No. 29), Rudolph Swoboda, Heinrich von Angeli and Laurits Tuxen, whose constant employment tended to annoy the British establishment.

Queen Victoria and Prince Albert did retain, however, some sympathy for certain British painters. The Queen was notably patient and considerate with Landseer, who was a slow worker and found it difficult to finish compositions. He was often overwrought and ultimately succumbed to a state of nervous depression that was only relieved later in life by heavy drinking, but the representation of his work in the Royal Collection is unsurpassed. Important and timely purchases by Queen Victoria of works by artists like W. P. Frith, the young Leighton, Roberts, Holl and Lady Butler (No. 30) were influential in the careers of these painters.

In all matters of art Queen Victoria was advised by her husband, Prince Albert. 'No other woman has the same . . . motive for being absolutely guided by the superior mind of her husband', wrote Lord Clarendon in December 1861, the very month of Prince Albert's death. The Prince was a great supporter of the arts in Britain, and as President of the Fine Arts Commission he initiated and developed some significant projects, such as the redecoration of the Houses of Parliament after the fire of 1834, the Great Exhibition of 1851 and the Art

Treasures exhibition held in Manchester in 1857. The refurbishing of the Houses of Parliament was to be carried out in fresco as part of a general revival of interest in earlier techniques, and the same medium was used for the decoration of the Garden Pavilion (demolished in 1928) in the grounds of Buckingham Palace, which involved several British artists working under the direction of Ludwig Grüner.

The enthusiasm that Queen Victoria and Prince Albert showed for the visual arts was given its greatest impetus at Osborne House and Balmoral Castle, which were both private residences where family life could be lived to the full. Numerous pictures were commissioned for these residences: portraits, genre scenes and landscapes – all often small in scale and intensely personal – by British and German artists. Several of the paintings commissioned or acquired were based on subjects inspired by literature. In this category works by John Martin, Daniel Maclise and W. E. Frost are the most distinguished. Prince Albert was very attentive to matters of interpretation, technique and drawing, and on occasions he would rather alarmingly watch while the artists painted. Frequently paintings were exchanged by Queen Victoria and Prince Albert as gifts on birthdays or at Christmas.

One area where Prince Albert's taste can be described as pioneering is his appreciation of early Italian, German and Netherlandish art. During the first half of the nineteenth century, the Nazarene artists from Germany had rediscovered Italian art of the fourteenth and fifteenth centuries and had made such painting the basis of their styles. The Scottish artist William Dyce, whose work Prince Albert admired and acquired, was an important point of contact between these developments and the Pre-Raphaelites in Britain, but for some reason Prince Albert failed to take proper advantage of this interest and did not add any major works by the Nazarenes to the collection. The largest group of early paintings acquired by Prince Albert, however, came somewhat unexpectedly. A German collector, Prince Ludwig Kraft Ernst Oettingen-Wallerstein, negotiated a private financial loan with Prince

Albert in 1847 and duly deposited his collection of Italian, German and Netherlandish primitives in London as surety. Prince Albert tried to sell the paintings on behalf of Prince Oettingen-Wallerstein but failed, so they came into his personal possession. The best pictures in the group were not retained for the collection and were given to the National Gallery by Queen Victoria after Prince Albert's death in 1861 in his memory. Even so, significant additions to the collection were made during this period in the 1840s, when works by Duccio, Bernardo Daddi, Gentile da Fabriano, Gozzoli and Justus of Ghent were purchased, some of which were hung in Osborne House in Prince Albert's Dressing and Writing-Room. These acquisitions are in marked contrast to others of a more traditional 'old master' flavour – Coello, Rubens, Vranx and Willaerts – which tend to be overlooked in any assessment of Queen Victoria's contribution to the Royal Collection.

After Prince Albert's death Queen Victoria tried to maintain the momentum that had been established in the early decades of the reign, but, though loyal to his intentions, it was a lonely task and opportunities for fresh thinking were lost. There are several paintings of the principal domestic celebrations of the Queen's reign (the Golden Jubilee of 1887 and the Diamond Jubilee of 1897), alongside depictions of significant events in imperial history. To these can be added pictures by Australian (for example, M. Claxton's *View of Sydney*) and Canadian artists (for example, landscapes by A. A. Edson, H. Watson and T. Martin) – these last acquired for Queen Victoria by her son-in-law, the Marquess of Lorne, while he was Governor-General (1878–1883).

A critic such as George Moore, who was in touch with developments in Paris and embraced modernist attitudes, was sorely depressed on viewing the paintings in *The Victorian Exhibition illustrating Fifty Years of Her Majesty's Reign 1837–1887*, held at the New Gallery in 1891–2 and to which Queen Victoria lent over fifty works. To him the royal pictures seemed boring, repetitive, bourgeois, altogether lacking in vision. He wrote that 'the middling from every country in Europe seems to have found a ready welcome at the Court of Queen Victoria', and he concluded, 'pity is that the private taste of Royalty creates the public taste of the nation'.

Yet against such judgments it has to be said that few monarchs cared so much for the presentation and upkeep of the Royal Collection. While Prince Albert was alive great efforts had been expended on the organization of the miniatures, drawings and prints, and the task of inventorying the pictures was begun afresh. Queen Victoria herself always remained conscious of her duty to preserve the Royal Collection according to the best standards of the day, and she thus has a worthy place in the hierarchy of royal collectors. As she wrote in her Journal (16 December 1842):

'Went to St George's Hall [Windsor Castle] to look at more old pictures, & the more I see them the more thunderstruck & shocked I am at the way in which the pictures, many fine ones amongst them, & of interesting value, have been thrown about & kept in lumber rooms at Hampton Court, whilst this Castle, and Buckingham Palace are literally without pictures. George III took the greatest care of all of them, George IV grew too ill to settle many things, except in the Corridor at Windsor Castle, and William IV, who was not famed for his good taste sent all the pictures away. My care, or rather more my dearest Albert's, for he delights in these things, will be to have them restored, to find places for them, and to prevent, as much as it is in our power, pictures of the Family, and others of interest and value from being thrown about again.'

Such aims would have impressed Charles I and, in so far as they are applicable today, underline the continuity that is one of the hallmarks of the Royal Collection.

PICTURES

The Royal Collection provides an invaluable introduction to several types of painting. No finer demonstration of the evolution of the state portrait, for example, could be devised. Introduced by the Tudors, it is a type of portraiture that is still of the greatest significance, even though as a whole the painted portrait has perhaps been forced to retreat before the shuttered lens of the ordinary camera and the zoom lens of the television camera. The state portrait has three purposes. First, the establishment of a dynasty and the recognition of a ruler's features. Such portraits ostensibly work in the same manner as icons, and they were frequently duplicated for widespread dispersal and consumption on an official basis. Second, state portraits were painted for diplomatic reasons, either in the context of marriage proposals or as a straightforward advocacy of foreign policy. Third, there was the exchange of portraits between royal families, many of which were interrelated by marriage. It was in these three ways that early picture galleries in royal palaces were stocked, appearing to the outsider as a visual representation of an impeccable pedigree.

The state portrait offers a considerable challenge to a painter who has to manipulate as convincingly as possible the conventions of grand full-length portraiture in a tradition inherited from the Renaissance. It has been hard to sustain this tradition, however, into the twentieth century, and contemporary painters struggle with the basic structure of the design or the freshness of touch that Van Dyck, Ramsay or Lawrence brought to the art of state portraiture. Added to this is the familiarity of the monarch's image in the modern world as a result of mass communication, so that the present-day portrait painter does not even have the chance to surprise or to engender excitement.

Nobody was more conscious of his own image than Henry VIII, and he was the first British sovereign to commission a life-size portrait for distribution at home and abroad. For this purpose he enlisted the help of Hans Holbein the Younger, who in 1537 painted the Whitehall Mural for the Privy Chamber at Whitehall Palace. The mural was lost in the fire of 1698, but the composition is preserved in a copy made in the seventeenth century by Remigius van Leemput (Fig. 4). The figure of Henry VIII on the left served as the prototype for the famous and much replicated full-length images of the King standing almost square on and looking directly out at the spectator. It can be appreciated immediately what a break with tradition such an image was, if it is remembered that a portrait of Henry V, which dates from early in Henry VIII's reign and forms part of a collection of likenesses of the King's forebears, depicts the King in profile, as on a portrait medal. Similarly, the power of Henry VIII's new image was readily acknowledged in so far as it was adopted in reverse for the King's son, the young and not so omnipotent Edward VI.

The icongraphy of Elizabeth I is as diverse and as fascinating as that of Queen Victoria. In both cases we can follow the transformation of a growing girl into a totem of semidivine imperial power. The portrait of the young Elizabeth I by an unknown painter (*c.* 1546), resplendent in her crimson dress and jewels, is the finest image of the Queen before the accession to the throne. She is shown holding a book, reminding us of the quality of her mind and the elegance of her deportment. The potency of the Queen as a figure of state is best represented on a panel by the Monogrammist HE entitled *Elizabeth I and the Three Goddesses* (Fig. 5). Here, standard Renaissance convention allows the Queen, equipped with the symbols of office, to play the role of Paris in judging the qualities of Juno, Pallas Minerva and Venus. The flattery is that Elizabeth I herself personifies all the attributes of the goddesses and so puts them to shame. The same visual progression occurs with Queen Victoria. There are several depictions of her as a girl, such as that by Richard Westall portraying her aged eleven holding a

FIG. 4 Remigius van Leemput (d.1675), *Henry VII and Elizabeth of York, Henry VIII and Jane Seymour* (after Hans Holbein the Younger). Oil on canvas, 1667.

sketchbook and accompanied by a pet dog. Soon this innocent figure was to be transformed into George Hayter's official state portrait, in which the Queen, still only eighteen years old, is seated on the throne wearing full regalia – an image as tried and tested as any, and one that goes back indeed to J. M. Wright's compelling rendering of Charles II.

It is true to say that state portraiture was radically improved by the arrival of Van Dyck on the scene. He first arrived in London to work for James I in 1620, when his fellow countrymen, Paul van Somer and Daniel Mytens, were serving as court painters. Van Somer's depiction of James I is stiff and undeniably awkward. Even though it may be an accurate portrait, it is unimaginative. Mytens, who was an extremely competent portrait painter, shows Charles I in a relaxed pose shortly after his accession, framed by a looped curtain before a balustrade, the

only suggestion of his status being the ribbon of the Order of the Garter. Van Dyck develops Mytens's formula by redeploying the props of kingship in a highly suggestive way. Paradoxically, the nonchalant pose and the laying aside of the crown, sceptre and orb makes the King far more impressively regal, and his status is reinforced by the column and the setting. The refinement and ability of the painter bring distinction to the King. The artist exercised these qualities on whatever scale he worked and on whatever type of composition he devised.

The new formulae that Van Dyck introduced into court portraiture provided subsequent painters with endless scope. If the course of the state portrait is pursued into the reign of George III and beyond, it can be seen how influential Van Dyck's example proved to be. On his accession in 1761 George III appointed the Scottish artist Allan Ramsay as court

FIG. 5 The Monogrammist HE (active 1560s),
Elizabeth I and the Three Goddesses.
Oil on panel, 1569.

painter. He produced the most sympathetic and most appropriate state portraits of the King and Queen Charlotte: in scale, colour, handling and pose these portraits match Van Dyck's achievements. They reveal the shyness and dignity that characterized George III and Queen Charlotte and encouraged them to lead their lives in a totally unpretentious way in close harmony with their numerous children. The portraits have elegantly staged scenes with sweeping curtains tied to columns, and they are painted in a soft powdered rococo range of colour inspired by contemporary French painting.

Later in his reign George III fell under the spell of Thomas Gainsborough, who towards the end of his life painted images of the King and Queen that are unsurpassed in the magic of the handling of the paint, the sense of majestic, easy movement and the almost tender relationship between artist and patron – a rapport that was not retained by the young Thomas Lawrence. It was, however, not difficult for a painter with the dexterity of Lawrence to capture the charm, enthusiasm and ebullience of George IV. Lawrence depicts a dashing, glittering display of robes and chains, symbolizing the florid, restless, overblown character beneath all the weight of cloth. Painting with unflagging panache and endless variety, the artist relates the King perfectly to that paradise of ormolu that he created around himself at Carlton House, the Royal Pavilion at Brighton and ultimately at Buckingham Palace and Windsor Castle. By contrast, it remained a perennial problem for artists to render the more ponderous virtues of William IV. At the beginning of this century Sir Luke Fildes, in his portraits of Edward VII and Queen Alexandra and subsequently of George V, and Sir Gerald Kelly, in his portraits of King George VI and Queen Elizabeth, were still working within the parameters established by Van Dyck as refined by eighteenth-century French artists.

Still, the very success of Van Dyck's renderings of the Stuart court rested on his ability to penetrate beneath the veneer of court life and to reveal the personalities so often obscured by protocol. Later artists may not have had the skill or insight to do this, but the domesticity of life in the royal family nonetheless became an accepted theme, especially with the Hanoverians. The painter who perfected the 'royal conversation piece' was a German artist from Frankfurt, Johann Zoffany. During the mid-1760s he painted Queen Charlotte with her two eldest children, George, Prince of Wales, and Frederick, Duke of York, in Buckingham House in a room overlooking the garden (Fig. 3). She is seated at her dressing table, while the children play around her. The artist has brought the picture to a high degree of finish, and it is replete with a number of crisply painted details, notably the reflections. There is, first of all, the reflection of the sharp profile of the Queen's own face seen in the mirror on the dressing table and then of the lady-in-waiting glimpsed in the other room. This informal impression of everyday life was carried through to Sir Edwin Landseer, who in 1845 painted *Windsor Castle in Modern Times* showing Queen Victoria with Prince Albert and the young Princess Victoria (the future Empress of Germany) surrounded by dogs and, perhaps rather incongruously, dead game that Prince Albert has just shot.

The theme of informality is best exemplified by the portraits of royal children. Again, it is Van Dyck who provides the starting point with the children of Charles I. Seemingly grouped together in artful insouciance and accompanied by pet dogs, the children beguile us with their privileged innocence, but such a description underestimates the skill with which the artist has invested small figures with a feeling of monumentality and paid close attention to the finery of their clothes. The secret of Van Dyck's success in this department is simple: he treats children like grown-ups. Zoffany, by contrast, goes to the opposite extreme, when during the mid-1760s he again shows George, Prince of Wales, and Frederick, Duke of York, but this time without the Queen. They are dressed in infants' 'coats' and besport themselves by a fire in a room in Buckingham House, which is suitably hung with pictures of royal or aristocratic children by Van Dyck.

Thirteen of the fifteen children of George III and Queen Charlotte were more memorably painted in a series of ovals by Gainsborough and exhibited at the Royal Academy in 1783. On a far grander scale is Copley's portrait of the three youngest daughters of George III painted two years later (No. 25). It was Winterhalter who returned to the theme of royal children when he was working for Queen Victoria and Prince Albert, bringing an immediacy of image and slickness of brushwork that makes the best of his portraits so winning.

There was, of course, a middle-ground between the official state portrait and the purely personal depiction of the sovereign's children, or the 'royal conversation piece'. This middle-ground is marked by the informal portrait of the monarch, not usually replicated for use in the public demesne. Such portraits are often in three-quarters length and were sometimes displayed in public at Royal Academy exhibitions but then retained by the sitters. The renderings by Zoffany of George III and Queen Charlotte in this manner possess the trappings of monarchy, but the poses are relaxed and somewhat off guard. Similarly, George IV when Prince of Wales preferred to have himself depicted by George Stubbs out riding by the Serpentine rather than in official robes, or by John Russell in the lurid green uniform of the royal Kentish Bowmen.

The whole gamut of private royal portraiture can be demonstrated by reference to Queen Victoria. In 1843 Winterhalter painted a head and shoulders of the young Queen Victoria, as a birthday surprise for Prince Albert. Indeed, its sheer abandoned sensuality comes as no less of a surprise for us today. Later, in 1850, Winterhalter painted the Queen with Prince Arthur as a baby on the terrace at Osborne House overlooking the Solent on a cloudless blue day. Even when Queen Victoria and Prince Albert went to costume balls, artists were on hand to record the event: Landseer shows them as Queen Philippa and Edward III, and Winterhalter as Restoration figures with Prince Albert rather proudly dressed as Charles II. This is history as a matter of dressing up, but such pleasures were not to last long, and after

Prince Albert's death the court became a place of leaden gloom. The most memorable image of the mourning Queen Victoria was painted in 1899 by Heinrich von Angeli, who succeeded Winterhalter as court artist and worked for the Queen for twenty-five years. She was particularly pleased by von Angeli's moving image, which combined the traditional pose representing grief and melancholy with the symbolism of the fading roses.

The recording of historical events and the personalities involved in them is another category in which the Royal Collection is rich. There are, for instance, two large paintings recording the meeting of Henry VIII with Francis I at the Field of the Cloth of Gold in 1520. In their emphasis on narrative the pictures provide a bare factual record of an important diplomatic occasion. The first painting represents the departure of the English King from Dover and the second the meeting itself near Calais. A change of pace is evident in Robert Streeter's *Boscobel House and Whiteladies*, which commemorates Charles II's escape from Cromwell's troops after the Battle of Worcester in 1651. This was not a very auspicious event, and for more worthy military occasions it is necessary to move forward to the eighteenth century.

Ironically, it was an American painter, Benjamin West, who in 1772 was appointed Historical Painter to George III, following his success with a set of pictures produced for the Warm Room in Buckingham House. The central paintings in this room were concerned with the theme of military valour, while the two overdoors provided examples of magnanimity. For these paintings West portrayed famous incidents from the classical past – *The Departure of Regulus*, *The Oath of Hannibal*, *The Death of Epaminondas* – but he also included the Renaissance with *The Death of Chevalier Bayard* and, more significantly, an event from his own day with *The Death of Wolfe* (Fig. 6), which occurred only twenty years earlier in 1759 in Canada during the Seven Years War. This last picture was a replica specially requested by the King of a composition (now in the National Gallery of Canada) originally

FIG. 6 Benjamin West (1728–1820), *The Death of Wolfe*.
Oil on canvas, 1771.

devised for Lòrd Grosvenor in the previous year.
West here paints a recent heroic death and in so
doing breaks with tradition by dressing the figures
in proper military uniforms, as opposed to antique
costume. West declared that 'the same truth that
guided the pen of the historian should govern the
pencil of the artist'. Even though the composition of
The Death of Wolfe is contrived (there are figures
who were not actually in attendance on Wolfe at his
death) and is dependent upon an established religious composition (*The Lamentation of Christ*), West
succeeds in conveying the squalor and agony of
contemporary war in the heroic mould. The fact
that similar scenes from the more distant past were
included in the same room sharpened people's
response to *The Death of Wolfe*, of which Sir Joshua

Reynolds said, 'I foresee that this picture will not
only become one of the most popular, but occasion
a revolution in art'. In terms of art *The Death of
Wolfe* is elevated to a level of idealized truth and as a
result appealed to George III, who had a very acute
sense of history.

This is also evident in West's next project
(1786–9) for the King, a series of paintings to adorn
the Audience Chamber in Windsor Castle. These
depicted events from the reign of Edward III and
culminated in *The Inauguration of the Order of the
Garter*, which was founded by Edward III in 1348
and is still closely associated with Windsor Castle.
The other pictures (several of very large dimensions)
comprise representations of Edward III and his son,
the Black Prince, during the Hundred Years War
against the French. For these incidents West referred
to Jean Froissart's *Chronicles* and David Hume's
History of England (1754–62) for the narrative flow,

but for details of arms, armour, flags and other accoutrements of war it is clear that the artist consulted antiquarian publications. These close links between West's paintings and antiquarian research demonstrate the renewal of interest in medieval history in late-eighteenth-century European art, but the large scale on which West conceived these scenes shows him to have been in the vanguard of the Gothic revival that both George III and George IV supported.

The fact that Edward III conducted a long and vigorous war against the French would have been an important consideration for George III, whose popularity increased during his reign as a direct result of the threat from external powers, particularly France. George III's patriotism, his sense of occasion, his accessibility, his attempt to be politically independent, even his longevity helped to unite the nation during the 1780s. West's portrait of George III, painted in 1779 when the country was threatened by invasion, captures this moment perfectly. It depicts the King in military uniform, leading the nation in the preparations for war: he holds a roll recording troop dispositions, his charger is restrained by a groom, his royal regalia is discarded, he is about to put on his military hat and mantle, while in the background the fleet and a regiment of Light Dragoons prepare for war. This was the period in which the regiments and uniforms of the British army were being standardized. Several artists were commissioned to paint regimental uniforms, but few reached the degree of precision that Stubbs brought to the Light Dragoons (No. 26). George IV when Prince of Wales was Colonel-Commandant of the Tenth Light Dragoons and was deeply attracted to its uniform, in which he was painted by Sir William Beechey.

Many other strands of royal activities and interests meet in George IV. He loved dressing up in special clothes and uniforms (he was always in debt to his tailor); he spent huge sums on uniforms, weapons and military equipment, as well as on works of art. There was in him, too, the love of female beauty that was anticipated by Charles II's court, displayed to such good effect in the series 'Windsor Beauties', painted by Sir Peter Lely in 1662–5 for Anne Hyde, the wife of the future James II. This memorable set was unjustly described by the early-nineteenth-century critic William Hazlitt as 'a set of kept mistresses, painted, tawdry, showing off their theatrical or meretricious airs and graces, without one touch of real elegance or refinement, or one spark of sentiment to touch the heart'. The series inspired the set by Sir Godfrey Kneller known as the 'Hampton Court Beauties', painted during the 1690s for Mary II and defined as portraits 'of the principal ladies attending upon Her Majesty, or who were frequently in her retinue'. William III hung them in The King's Private Dining Room in Hampton Court Palace.

The Hanoverians, by contrast, preferred to record military and naval commanders – Cornwallis, Hastings, Granby, Southampton, Keppel, Rodney, St Vincent, Nelson – or the exploits in which they participated. The most elaborate series of this *exemplum virtutis* is displayed in the Waterloo Chamber in Windsor Castle. This set of portraits was commissioned by George IV and carried out by Thomas Lawrence over several years after 1814, but the paintings were not installed until the early 1830s during the reign of William IV. The effect of the Waterloo Chamber, which celebrates the defeat of Napoleon I by the Allies, is daunting, and the room features one of the greatest portraits of the Romantic period – Pope Pius VII.

The widest range of historical incident as pictorial representation, however, dates from the reign of Queen Victoria. Artists, such as Wilkie, Leslie, Hayter and the Dane, Laurits Tuxen, were enlisted to portray moments of personal significance in her reign and later the family events that seemed to be so numerous and densely populated. Such pictures provide a contrast to the isolation of her widowhood. The Queen enjoyed having her pets painted, as well as members of the Royal Household or people she admired at home or abroad. Highlights in her reign are recorded with punctilious accuracy. Artists were on hand to record State Visits between

France and Britain, and political developments in India. In his rendering of the opening of the Great Exhibition of 1851, for example, David Roberts showed the interior of the Crystal Palace, while Winterhalter in his *First of May* (No. 29) alludes to the same event by representing the Crystal Palace in the background, seen over the shoulder of its creator. The presence of the Duke of Wellington is a reminder that Queen Victoria was immensely proud of her country's military achievements, although attitudes to war were changing, as perhaps can be detected in *The Roll Call* by Lady Butler (no. 30).

Queen Victoria and Prince Albert acquired Balmoral Castle in Scotland in 1848 and used it as a private retreat where the Queen could sketch and Prince Albert hunt. Field sports have been a traditional pastime through the ages. An early representation by Robert Peake the Elder depicts Henry, Prince of Wales, in the hunting field (No. 3), whereas John Wootton (No. 18) shows the early Hanoverians hunting in the Thames Valley near Henley. It was George IV, however, who commissioned the finest equestrian paintings in the Royal Collection from Sawrey Gilpin, George Stubbs and Ben Marshall. This tradition was continued by Queen Victoria, who commissioned works from J. F. Herring, but she also employed Sir Edwin Landseer, who was the outstanding animal painter of his day. The Royal Collection has a wide-ranging representation of Landseer's depictions of animals, extending from domestic pets, such as *Eos* (Fig. 7), through tamed animals (*Isaac von Amburgh and his Animals*, 1839) to the wildlife of Scotland, where the Highlands proved to be a source of inspiration for artist and patron alike. Landseer's skills lay not only in the accuracy of his drawing, which like Stubbs was based on dissection, but on the vivid characterization of the animals and the ability to incorporate them into narrative compositions. The artist also had the opportunity to paint an official equestrian portrait of the young Queen Victoria, thereby attempting to emulate those of Charles I by Van Dyck. Landseer made several oil studies for

FIG. 7 Sir Edwin Landseer (1803–1873), *Eos*. Oil on canvas, 1841.

this important and challenging commission that dragged on for some thirty years, but in the end, as on other occasions, his nerve failed him, and the project was left unfinished.

PALACES

The paintings in the Royal Collection have always been widely distributed through many buildings. Different monarchs preferred different residences, and the pictures were often moved about in accordance with such preferences. Charles I hung the bulk of his collection in Whitehall Palace. William III and Mary II placed the emphasis on Hampton Court Palace and Kensington Palace. George III moved important elements of the collection into Buckingham House after he purchased it in 1762. George IV concentrated his collection in Carlton House until 1827, when he had the house pulled down and began to develop Windsor Castle and to transform Buckingham House into a palace. Queen Victoria disliked Hampton Court Palace and soon abandoned Kensington Palace, where she had been brought up as a child, favouring Buckingham Palace, Windsor Castle, Osborne House and Balmoral Castle. Although the British Court is designated as the Court of St James's, the palace itself is associated mainly with the Tudor and Stuart dynasties. The Hanoverians abandoned it as a royal residence and tended to use the palace more for formal court proceedings such as levées and the reception of heads of state. Since Queen Victoria, Buckingham Palace has become associated in public consciousness as the principal residence of the monarch and as the hub of the Court of St James's.

The documentary basis for the Royal Collection is the series of inventories listing the paintings in the various palaces, but in addition there are several written accounts incorporated in diaries, memoirs or early forms of travel literature. Diplomatic ambassadors or distinguished visitors sometimes noted what they saw. Even if the information is inaccurate or piecemeal, the vividness of an eye-witness account is often compelling, as in Baron Waldstein's description of Whitehall Palace, which

he visited in 1600. The genre of travel literature, as practised by Celia Fiennes (1662–1741) and Daniel Defoe (1660–1731), for example, provides information on royal palaces but in the context of the traveller moving through the countryside.

The eighteenth century was the age of the antiquarian. The finest account of the collection of Frederick, Prince of Wales, was written by George Vertue, while a hastier but no less instructive description of Buckingham House was written by Horace Walpole after visits he made in 1782 and 1783. Walpole's account can, in fact, be corroborated by the schematic drawings made of the pictures as they were arranged in 1774, after the house had been remodelled by Sir William Chambers. During the nineteenth century, with the emergence of art-historical scholarship and with certain palaces – especially Hampton Court – becoming more accessible, more considered listings of the paintings were prepared in the form of straightforward catalogues. J. D. Passavant, a Nazarene painter and an outstanding Raphael scholar who later became Director of the Städelsches Kunstinstitut in Frankfurt, was the first in this field with *Tour of a German Artist in England . . .* (1836), and he was followed by the first Director of the Royal Museum in Berlin, G. F. Waagen, who published *Works of Art and Artists in England* (1838) and *Treasures of Art in Great Britain* (1854). Comparable with these was Anna Jameson's *Companion to the Most Celebrated Private Galleries of Art in London* (1844), which, as far as the Royal Collection is concerned, was based on the holdings in Buckingham Palace but also included the Grand Corridor in Windsor Castle. In the same volume Jameson published descriptions of other important collections in London – in Bridgewater House, Stafford House, Grosvenor House and Lansdowne House.

Balancing this body of literature is visual material indicating how and where the paintings were arranged in the various palaces. The most elaborate of these is the three-volume publication by William Henry Pyne, *The History of the Royal Residences . . .* (1819), which contains colour engravings of several

FIG. 8 Charles Wild (1781–1835), *The Blue Velvet Room: Carlton House*. Watercolour, *c.* 1818. For W. H. Pyne, *The History of the Royal Residences . . .* (1819).

FIG. 9 Joseph Nash (1809–1878), *Windsor Castle: The Corridor, South*. Watercolour, *c.* 1840. For J. Nash, *Views of the Interior and Exterior of Windsor Castle* (1848).

rooms in each of the main buildings, together with verbal descriptions. In the case of Carlton House the illustrations are a unique record of the interiors of what in its time was one of the most lavishly decorated palaces in Europe (Fig. 8). Although Pyne included Windsor Castle in his volumes, Joseph Nash published another set of colour engravings of the Castle in 1848 (*Views of the Interior and Exterior of Windsor Castle*), after the refurbishment undertaken by George IV; they include the Grand Corridor (Fig. 9), The Queen's Ballroom and the Waterloo Chamber. These images, however, were soon to be supplanted by photography. The changes made in the hang of the Picture Gallery in Buckingham Palace during the reign of George V, for example, are recorded in photographs (Fig. 10).

Modern technology has recently allowed a further advance in cataloguing of the Royal Collection, namely the computer. Curatorial information on all the paintings and miniatures has in the last few years been put on computer, and eventually the whole of the Royal Collection, including sculpture, furniture, porcelain, drawings and prints, will be entered in the same way. Whatever the means, the overall duties that Charles I requested his first Surveyor, Abraham van der Doort, to perform following his

FIG. 10 *Buckingham Palace: The Picture Gallery, c.* 1915.

appointment in 1625, have not really changed to this day. These were 'to prevent and keepe them [the paintings] (soe much as in him lyeth) from being spoiled or defaced, to order marke and number them, and to keepe a Register of them, to receive and deliver them, and likewise to take order for the makeing and coppying of Pictures as Wee [Charles I] or the Lord Chamberlaine of Our Household shall directe, And to this end . . . hee shall have Accesse at Convenient Times unto Our Galleries Chamber and other Roomes where Our Pictures are'.

THE CATALOGUE

NOTE

The paintings are arranged in chronological order. The commentaries are intended to place the paintings in a general context regarding the artist's oeuvre and the history of royal collectors.

Bibliographical references are limited in the main to the officially published catalogues of the Royal Collection (see List of Abbreviations) in which full citations of earlier literature, exhibitions and provenance may be found, as well as more closely argued reasons for dating, details of different versions and other such related matters. Only the most important references to a painting, during or since the publication of the relevant catalogue, have been added. A few paintings included in this exhibition have not yet been officially catalogued, and in such cases the references should be regarded as summary. A list of titles (including other official catalogues not in the List of Abbreviations) for further reading on the Royal Collection is given on p. 95.

LIST OF ABBREVIATIONS

Millar, 1963
O. Millar, *The Tudor, Stuart and Early Georgian Pictures in the Collection of Her Majesty the Queen*, London, 1963.

Millar, 1969
O. Millar, *The Later Georgian Pictures in the Collection of Her Majesty The Queen*, London, 1969.

White, 1982
C. White, *The Dutch Pictures in the Collection of Her Majesty The Queen*, Cambridge University Press, 1982.

Shearman, 1983
J. Shearman, *The Early Italian Pictures in the Collection of Her Majesty The Queen*, Cambridge University Press, 1983.

Levey, 1991
M. Levey, *The Later Italian Pictures in the Collection of Her Majesty The Queen*, 2nd edition, Cambridge University Press, 1991.

Lloyd, 1991
C. Lloyd, *The Queen's Pictures: Royal Collectors through the Centuries*, Catalogue by Christopher Lloyd with an essay by Sir Oliver Millar, National Gallery Publications, London, 1991.

Millar, 1992
O. Millar, *The Victorian Pictures in the Collection of Her Majesty The Queen*, Cambridge University Press, 1992.

1

JACOPO DAL PONTE, *called* BASSANO

c . 1 5 1 0 — 1 5 9 2

J acopo Bassano was born in the small town of Bassano del Grappa, situated about thirty miles to the north-west of Venice, close to the Dolomite mountains. He was the most famous representative of a dynasty of painters founded by his father Francesco dal Ponte, with whom he often worked on a collaborative basis. Bassano del Grappa owed allegiance to Venice, and it is with such painters as Titian, Veronese and Tintoretto that Jacopo Bassano is ultimately most closely associated. From provincial beginnings the artist gradually developed an independent style that was influenced not only by Venetian painting but by the Mannerism of central Italian painters and by knowledge of work by German and Netherlandish artists. The most innovative aspect of Jacopo Bassano's work, however, was his treatment of subject matter. Although he rarely depicted mythological scenes, Bassano's religious paintings were famous in his own day for their pastoral qualities and for the emphasis on genre. There are also a number of nocturnal scenes dating from the second half of his long working life, when, like Renoir in a later century, his output was affected by blindness.

The *Adoration of the Shepherds* dates from a period between such works as the *Adoration of the Magi* (*c.* 1542) in Edinburgh (National Gallery of Scotland) and the *Rest on the Flight into Egypt* (*c.* 1547) in Milan (Pinacoteca Ambrosiana). Another painting of the *Adoration of the Shepherds* executed *c.* 1545 (Venice, Gallerie dell'Accademia, formerly Giusti del Giardino Collection, Verona), has several compositional features in common with the present picture. The 1540s was the decade during which the artist's personality began to emerge, even though several influences can still be detected in his work.

Bassano's starting point for the composition was the

The Adoration of the Shepherds

c. 1546
Oil on canvas
139.5 × 219 cm

painting of the same subject by Titian executed for the Duke of Urbino in 1532–4. This painting may be the panel now in Florence (Palazzo Pitti), but Bassano's source was the woodcut after it by the Master I.B, who has been identified as Giovanni Boitto. On the other hand, the architectural features and the shepherd playing the bagpipes recall the woodcut of the *Nativity* by Albrecht Dürer from the *Little Passion* (1511). In this *Adoration of the Shepherds*, therefore, Bassano has skilfully fused these diverse sources into a large-scale composition based on a pyramidal grouping with the Virgin and Child centrally positioned. The figures are firmly and sympathetically drawn with a surprising degree of realism. There is a wide range of colours in the draperies extending from warm earthy tones to the *changeant* qualities of the violet (St Joseph), amaranth and blue (the kneeling shepherd), and the pink and sulphur yellow (the bagpiper).

Iconographically, it is noteworthy that the broken elements of classical architecture refer to the passing of the Old Law, which will be replaced by the New Law symbolized by the Christ Child. The tree, which is about to be nibbled by the goat, prefigures the Passion of Christ, emphasizing the role of Christ as Redeemer. While the figures in the foreground dominate the composition, the landscape background is important in that it provides a pastoral setting. The town on the hill at the foot of the mountain is Bassano del Grappa.

The *Adoration of the Shepherds* almost certainly belonged to Charles I, who was a great admirer of Venetian painting.

FROM HAMPTON COURT PALACE
REFERENCES: Shearman, 1983, No. 16; Lloyd, 1991, No. 7; *Jacopo Bassano c. 1510–1592*, ed. B. L. Brown and P. Marini, Bassano del Grappa and Fort Worth, 1992, pp. 72–3 and No. 17.

2

ANNIBALE CARRACCI

1560–1609

T he painter was the most influential member of a family of artists from Bologna who created a watershed in the development of Italian painting. Together with his elder brother Agostino (1557–1602) and following the lead of his cousin Ludovico (1555–1619), Annibale Carracci initiated a style that was seen not only as a revival of the High Renaissance but as a touchstone for the new century. He revitalized tradition and yet in doing so created a revolution. This new style was evolved in Bologna, but it was tested and proved to be triumphant in Rome in the frescoes undertaken for Cardinal Odoardo Farnese, begun in 1595 and finished in 1604–5. Until the end of the eighteenth century, the frescoes in the Palazzo Farnese were regarded as being equal in importance to works by Raphael and Michelangelo in Rome. In effect, Carracci redefined the meaning of the word classicism by combining the inheritance of the High Renaissance with the observation of reality. From Bologna the Carracci had examined afresh the work of Correggio in Parma and Titian, Tintoretto and Veronese in Venice. This resulted in a series of important large-scale altarpieces that swept aside the vestiges of Mannerism. On reaching Rome, Annibale Carracci was able to observe at first hand the legacy of antiquity, Raphael and Michelangelo. This brought about the formation of his mature style, characterized by a greater monumentality in the figures and more open, free-flowing rhythms. This style was of such dramatic import that it can only be referred to as a new grand manner. The Palazzo Farnese was, in essence, the training ground for painters of the next generation, such as Domenichino, Lanfranco, Guercino and Reni. During his final years, however, Annibale Carracci was struck by a curious, undiagnosed illness, and he was unable to paint.

Head of a Man in Profile

c. 1585
Oil on canvas
44.8 × 32.1 cm

The artist concerned himself not only with mythology in his frescoes and religious subjects in his altarpieces. There was also a pronounced secular element in his work. He painted landscapes, executed genre scenes and drew caricatures. Drawing was the basis of the Carraccis' new style, and the private 'academy' they formed in Bologna *c.* 1582, with its emphasis on drawing from life, was considered progressive. It was here that the artificial style of Mannerism was overthrown. *Head of a Man in Profile* is an oil sketch that was no doubt painted in such surroundings. The freedom in the handling of paint, the bold characterization and the spontaneity all derive from direct observation in an intimate atmosphere. It has been observed of Annibale Carracci that 'the formal side of his art had an interesting counterpart of informality', and his portraits attest this assertion. They are varied in style and are difficult to date. Indeed, they do not seem to form a coherent element within the artist's oeuvre. The present example has been dated 1585–90 and *c.* 1590, but it may be even earlier, perhaps contemporary with *The Butcher's Shop* (Oxford, Christ Church), which is normally dated *c.* 1582–3. What is certain is that the impact of this small portrait transcends its own century, and it may be equated with nineteenth-century French art, as exemplified by Thomas Couture or Manet.

The portrait is first recorded in the reign of George III, but it may have been acquired by his father, Frederick, Prince of Wales.

FROM HAMPTON COURT PALACE
REFERENCES: *Treasures from the Royal Collection*, The Queen's Gallery, Buckingham Palace, 1988, No. 55; Levey, 1991, No. 435.

3

ROBERT PEAKE THE ELDER

active 1576–1616

Henry, Prince of Wales, was the eldest son of James I and Anne of Denmark. He was born in 1594 at Stirling Castle in Scotland and died of typhoid fever in 1612 at the age of eighteen in St James's Palace. He had been formally created Prince of Wales in 1610, and on his death his younger brother Charles officially became heir-apparent in 1616, succeeding his father as Charles I in 1625.

Contemporaries had no doubt about the physical, intellectual and courtly virtues of Henry, Prince of Wales, and the funeral orations were unusually poignant. For many the range of his abilities, the breadth of his interests, and his defence of Protestantism revived memories of Elizabeth I's reign, but his achievements as collector and patron were in fact more in line with those of the Holy Roman Emperor, Rudolf II, in Prague and the Medici Grand Dukes in Florence, so that within a short space of time there was a late flowering of Renaissance and Mannerist culture in England. Artists of the calibre of Inigo Jones and Isaac Oliver, as well as writers like Ben Jonson, were key figures in the circle of Henry, Prince of Wales, who also employed artists from throughout Europe.

By European standards painting at the court of James I was not advanced. The principal portraitists were John de Critz and Robert Peake, who in 1610 was appointed joint Serjeant Painter to the King with de Critz and Gheeraedts the Younger, who was de Critz's brother-in-law. These painters had been trained at the end of Elizabeth I's reign and were subject to the influence of Netherlandish art. Their portraits are often formulaic, flat, two-dimensional images tending towards the decorative with little attempt at modelling or variety in the treatment of light. Peake seems to have been given responsibility for painting official images of Prince Henry, and there are several portraits by his hand, in addition to payments

Henry, Prince of Wales, in the Hunting-Field

c. 1605
Oil on canvas
190.5 × 165.1 cm

for other work dating from 1608 to 1611–12.

Peake used the present composition twice; first, for a painting dated 1604 (New York, Metropolitan Museum of Art), in which the Prince of Wales is attended by John, second Baron Harington of Exton (1592–1614): and, second, for the present painting, in which, apart from variations in the landscape, Henry is attended by Robert Devereux, third Earl of Essex (1591–1646), the son of Elizabeth I's favourite. Both paintings depict the Prince hunting. Other portraits of the Prince of Wales by Peake – one showing him as the warrior prince (Turin, Palazzo Chiablese) and another of him on horse-back (Parham Park) – are slightly later in date. Whatever European influences he absorbed, Peake also worked within the tradition of Nicholas Hilliard. The emphasis on line, the pastel colours, the blandness of the flesh tones and the detailed landscape settings are the recognizable traits of Peake's art.

The iconography of the portrait is also significant, since Henry, Prince of Wales, is depicted carrying out a particular task in accordance with the rules of hunting described in *Turbervile's Booke of Hunting* (1575). After the deer has been slain by the hounds, there is the distribution of the meat. This is initiated by the Prince, who dismounts and makes a gash in the neck extending to the belly to reveal the thickness and texture of the flesh. The Prince is shown here sheathing his sword, leaving the separation of the various parts of the deer to others. It is possible that Peake knew of the woodcuts illustrating *Turbervile's Booke of Hunting*.

FROM WINDSOR CASTLE

REFERENCES: Millar, 1963, No. 100; Roy Strong, *The English Icon*, London and New York, 1969, p. 20 and No. 222; Julius Held, *Rubens and his Circle: Studies by Julius S. Held*, ed. A. W. Lowenthal, D. Rosand, J. Walsh, Princeton University Press, 1982, 'Le Roi à la Chasse', pp. 70–72 (first published 1958); Roy Strong, *Henry, Prince of Wales and England's Lost Renaissance*, London, 1986, pp. 114–15.

4

CRISTOFANO ALLORI

1577–1621

The artist was the son of Alessandro Allori, who was the adopted son of Agnolo Bronzino, the court painter in Florence to Duke Cosimo I de' Medici and Eleanora of Toledo. Bronzino was one of the principal exponents of the Mannerist style, and he was in turn followed by his pupil Alessandro Allori. Cristofano Allori, however, rejected Mannerism, and with several artists of the younger generation in Florence he evolved a more restrained and realistic approach more suitable for the painting of religious narratives. Jacopo di Empoli, Gregorio Pagani and Ludovico Cigoli adopted similar styles, but the best known figure is Carlo Dolci (1616–1686), whose work was particularly sought after by British collectors during the eighteenth century.

Cristofano Allori was elected a member of the prestigious Accademia del Disegno in Florence in 1613 and held the political position of *podestà* for Pontedera in 1606. In his *Notizie de' professori del disegno da Cimabue in qua* ... (1681) Filippo Baldinucci describes the artist as a libertine who was given to occasional bouts of excessive piety. The present painting is a good example of Allori's proclivities and has been described as one of the most celebrated Florentine pictures of the seventeenth century.

There are, in fact, numerous versions of *Judith with the Head of Holofernes* painted for patrons in Rome and Florence. The best version is that in the Palazzo Pitti, Florence, executed for the Grand Duke Cosimo III in 1620, but the primacy of the picture in the Royal Collection can be deduced from the changes Allori made on the

Judith with the Head of Holofernes

1613
Oil on canvas
120.4 × 100.3 cm
Inscribed on the end of the bed, lower right: *Hoc Cristofori Allori/Bronzinii opere natura/hactenus invicta pene/vincitur Anno 1613*: This [work is] of Cristoforo [sic] Allori Bronzino, hitherto unvanquished, [he] has almost been defeated by the labour [of] painting, in the year 1613.

canvas as he worked (perhaps alluded to in the inscription), by the strong characterization and by the vivid colouring. This much was established when the painting was cleaned in 1978.

The story of Judith is recorded in the book of that name in the Apocrypha. A young and beautiful widow of great piety, she saves the besieged city of Bethulia from the Assyrians by going to the camp of Holofernes, the invading general, to entertain him. Having made Holofernes drunk, Judith decapitates him and carries his head back in a bag to Bethulia. According to Baldinucci, the figure of Judith in this painting is a portrait of the artist's lover, Maria di Giovanni Mazzafirra (died 1617).

The servant is a portrait of the lover's mother, and the features of the decapitated Holofernes are those of the artist himself. The painting, therefore, would seem to depict an unhappy liaison and illustrates the suffering experienced by Allori. The double meaning is corroborated in a poem (*La Galleria*) written by Giovanbattista Marino in Paris in 1619 on viewing one of Allori's versions of the composition. The theme was later developed by John Keats in *La Belle Dame sans Merci* (1819). Contemporary artists, like Jacopo Ligozzi, Lavinia Fontana and Artemisia Gentileschi, also introduced similar autobiographical elements into depictions of this subject, as did Caravaggio in the context of David and Goliath (Rome, Galleria Borghese).

The picture was most probably acquired by Charles I in 1625–7 from the Gonzaga collection in Mantua.

FROM HAMPTON COURT PALACE
REFERENCES: Shearman, 1983, No. 2; Lloyd, 1991, No. 23.

5

HENDRICK TER BRUGGHEN

c.1588–1629

The artist embarked upon his career in Utrecht, studying with Abraham Bloemart, but he spent ten influential years (1604–1614) in Rome, where he became versed in the style and subject matter of paintings by Caravaggio and his followers. Indeed, Ter Brugghen was one of the first Dutch artists to transmit the Caravaggesque style back to the north, where with Gerrit van Honthorst and Dirck Baburen he evolved a tenebrist manner of painting. Though shortlived, it was nonetheless an important moment in the development of seventeenth-century Dutch art, especially in the town of Delft. The chief characteristic of the style is the sharp contrast between light and shadow, evidenced here in the face of the sitter. The style lent itself to dramatic interpretations of religious, mythological and literary subjects, all of which were incorporated in Ter Brugghen's oeuvre. The treatment of light is especially significant, as it combines the emotive force found in Caravaggio's work with the more descriptive qualities associated with Dutch artists working later in the century. To this extent the present painting represents a slight waning of the influence of Caravaggio, and this is also apparent in the more unified tones the artist has used for the draperies.

Consistent with most of Ter Brugghen's output, however, is the bold composition, strong characterization and somewhat earthy subject matter. Although no doubt inspired in part by the itinerant musicians that were to be

A Laughing Bravo with a Bass Viol and a Glass

1625
Oil on canvas
104.8 × 85.1 cm
Signed upper left: *H T Brugghen
fecit 1625* (H T B in monogram)

seen in the Netherlands during the early seventeenth century, the painting could easily be interpreted as an allegory of the senses, specifically of sound (represented by the bass viol) and taste (symbolized by the contents of the glass). Alternatively, Ter Brugghen might have meant the picture to illustrate the theme of *vanitas*, whereby the brevity of song can be equated with the transience of life. The artist often depicted musicians in the context of such themes, but he only seems to have selected a bass viol for this purpose on one other occasion. The figure is invested with a certain brio. The model is found in several of Ter Brugghen's paintings, while the costume – including cap, feather, badge and the glass – are his standard studio properties. The relatively free handling of paint is in striking contrast with the care taken over the drawing (note particularly the still-life objects) and the skilful foreshortening. One authority on the artist also drew attention to the sitter's forced smile, comparing it to 'that thrown by the politician to his constituents' in 'a joyless wish to please'.

The painting was acquired by Charles I and sold after his execution in 1649, when it was purchased by the artist Sir Peter Lely, who returned it to the Royal Collection at the Restoration.

FROM HAMPTON COURT PALACE

REFERENCES: White, 1982, No. 33; Benedict Nicolson, *Caravaggism in Europe*, 2nd edition Turin, 1989, p. 194; Lloyd, 1991, No. 27.

6

F R A N S   H A L S

1 5 8 1 / 2 – 1 6 6 6

Hals stands second only to Rembrandt in the development of Dutch painting. Although he lived to be a considerable age and although his style is so vibrant, Hals was in fact not a prolific painter. His oeuvre is dominated by portraiture, and his few genre paintings and even rarer religious works seem to be little more than veiled portraits. However, his contribution to portrait painting was of the greatest significance and somewhat surprising, given that his artistic origins lay in the work of Karel van Mander and the death throes of late Mannerism, characterized by high-pitched colours and elaborate, over-dressed compositions.

Hals recorded the emergence of the Dutch Republic through his paintings. His portraits of individuals are notable for their confidence and the informality of the sitters, while the group portraits of militiamen and officials (nine were painted between 1616 and 1664) depict a growing emergence of corporate identity. In addition to these different types of portraiture was the technique. The sense of the momentary or the instantaneous was achieved not only by the pose or the expression but by the handling of the paint. The vitality of Hals's portraits is matched by a style of impulsive brushwork comprising loose, broken, angular, seemingly disconnected strokes. The brushwork really only coalesces when seen from a distance, and it always retains its *alla-prima* effect. Only Rembrandt and Velásquez, amongst contemporaries, could match Hals's dazzling display of visual pyrotechnics. It was this aspect of his work, quite apart from biographical considerations or any misunderstanding about subject matter, that appealed to nineteenth-century

Portrait of a Man

1630
Oil on canvas
116.1 × 90.1 cm
Inscribed upper right: *AETAT SUAE 36/AN.1630*

French painters, such as Gustave Courbet and Manet.

Portrait of a Man was painted at the height of the artist's powers. A change in Hals's style occurred in the 1630s, when his portraits show a greater simplicity and tonal unity. Figures are usually placed before plain backgrounds and dressed in clothes of sombre hues in accordance with fashion; the mood is subdued and characterization restrained. The portraits, however, are no less vivid and zestful, it is just that the results are obtained by different means. The monochromatic effect creates an atmospheric quality and the plain background a sense of spaciousness. There is a feeling of grandeur, but at three-quarters length it is presented on a scale that does not so much emphasize the sitter's status as his humanity. The figure seems to grow in stature, as if emerging out of the lower edge of the frame, while the corporeality is suggested by the jutting elbow and extended hand holding the glove, accentuated by the tautness of the clothes highlighted in broad brushstrokes. The flesh tones of the face and hands, and the details of the clothing like ruff, glove, and cuffs are aspects of the drawing as well as of visual emphasis. The figure is firmly pinioned to the surface as though being held specifically for the viewer to inspect him. Hals had no equal in making the impermanent permanent or in rendering the mobile immobile.

Portrait of a Man is first recorded in Buckingham House during the reign of George III, but it is more likely to have been acquired by his father, Frederick, Prince of Wales.

FROM BUCKINGHAM PALACE

REFERENCES: White, 1982, No. 56; Seymour Slive, *Frans Hals*, Royal Academy of Arts, London, 1989, No. 38.

7

ARTEMISIA GENTILESCHI

1593–1652

Self-Portrait as the Allegory of Painting

c. 1630
Oil on canvas
96.5 × 73.7 cm
Signed on the table in the centre:
A.G.F.

Artemisia Gentileschi was a painter of considerable renown in her own day, but her reputation evaporated soon after her death and has only recently been re-established. The daughter of a painter Orazio Gentileschi (1563–1639), she worked in Rome, Florence and Naples for extensive periods, as well as in Genoa and Venice. In 1638 she followed her father to London, where she most probably assisted him in painting the *Allegory of Peace and the Arts under the English Crown* for Henrietta Maria, the wife of Charles I, in the Queen's House at Greenwich. The artist resided in England until *c.* 1641. Charles I owned at least three paintings by her, including this *Self-Portrait*.

The primary influence on Artemisia Gentileschi's style was that of her father, whose mature work was dominated by the impact of Caravaggio. The vivid contrasts of light and shadow, the rich colouring, the choice of violent subject matter and the predilection for genre scenes are derived from Caravaggio in a general sense, but dissipated by Italian regional influences and the presence of northern European artists on the peninsular. The primary exponents of this style at the English Court were Gerrit van Honthorst and Orazio and Artemisia Gentileschis. The degree of realism with which Artemisia Gentileschi treated such themes as Judith, David and Goliath, and St John the Baptist is startling, just as there is a significant underlying tension in her paintings of Susannah and the Elders or Joseph and Potiphar's Wife. It is clear, however, that the artist's own life was not free from violence, and the long running trial in 1612 that sought to establish that the young Artemisia had been raped by the painter Agostino Tassi provides an abundance of evidence for the more tragic aspects of life in Rome during the early seventeenth century.

Although the *Self-Portrait* belonged to Charles I, it may not have been commissioned by him. Indeed, a portrait painted by Artemisia Gentileschi as early as 1630 for the famous antiquarian Cassiano dal Pozzo (1588–1657) may be the same self-portrait referred to later in a letter of 1637. It appears that this painting was never delivered to dal Pozzo, and it is possible that the artist brought it with her to London, where it was acquired by the King.

Unlike the famous *Self-Portrait* by Rubens that had been presented to Charles I *c.* 1623, Artemisia Gentileschi's painting is couched in allegorical terms based on the personification of Painting recorded in the *Iconologia* by Cesare Ripa (1611). For Ripa, Painting is a figure with dishevelled hair wearing brightly coloured drapery with a gold chain and a medallion in the form of a mask. Compared, for instance, with the *Self-Portrait* by Rubens in which the artist extols his social status, Artemisia Gentileschi here depicts herself in the act of painting as though eager to demonstrate her practical skills. This characterization is enhanced by the pose with the figure viewed from below, placed on a steep diagonal while working on a canvas, and also by the sharply lit flesh tones with the face almost in full profile. Painting is thus seen as a combination of intellectual allusion and sustained application – a powerful and telling statement if the social position of the female artist in the seventeenth century is taken into account.

FROM HAMPTON COURT PALACE
REFERENCES: M. D. Garrard, *Artemisia Gentileschi: The Image of the Female Hero in Italian Baroque Art*, Princeton University Press, 1989, pp. 85–88, 337–70; Benedict Nicolson, *Caravaggism in Europe*, 2nd edition, Turin, 1989, p. 111; Levey, 1991, No. 409; Lloyd, 1991, No. 13.

8

ATTRIBUTED TO LOUIS LE NAIN

1600/10−1648

The Young Card-Players

c. 1630–40
Oil on canvas
54.9 × 63.8 cm

The painting was acquired at auction in London by George IV, when it was stated to have come from the Palazzo Aldobrandini in Rome. Having been sold by the Roman dealer Castiglione to Thomas Lister Parker, the picture came into the possession of Walsh Porter (died 1809), a writer and collector who advised George IV on matters of art and played an important role in the furnishing and decoration of Carlton House. When Walsh Porter sold the picture at Christie's in 1803, it was described with a fair degree of accuracy as an 'exquisite jewel'.

The work of the three Le Nain brothers is difficult to disentangle, and the attribution of individual paintings to one or other of them is still the subject of debate. Of the three brothers both Antoine and Louis were born *c.* 1600–10, but it is believed that Antoine was the elder; both died in 1648. Matthieu was the youngest brother (born *c.* 1607) and lived longest (died 1677). All three were born in Laon but in 1629 had settled permanently in Paris, where they became founding members of the Académie des Beaux-Arts in 1648. Matthieu achieved notable success in the Paris art world, being referred to in 1652 as *peintre du roi*. Ultimately, he seems to have become a landowner, buying a farm near Laon, and was connected with the Paris militia, as a result of which he was ennobled.

In his *Le Galanteries de la cour* (1644) the contemporary writer Du Bail refers to three brothers as painters usually identified as the 'Le Nain'. He describes Antoine as a painter of 'miniatures and portraits in small'; Louis, who made 'Little pictures in which a thousand different attitudes which he copies from nature attract the eye'; and Matthieu is cited as a specialist in 'portraits and big pictures'. Faced with a paucity of information and several paintings, art historians have therefore been much exercised by the problems of attribution and dating. *The Young Card-Players*, for instance, has often been attributed to Matthieu Le Nain, but recently Louis has been suggested.

The appreciation of the work of the Le Nain, like that of Vermeer or Georges de la Tour, is a modern phenomenon. Despite gaining respect in their own day for paintings of religious and mythological subjects, as well as portraits, it is the genre paintings that have been given greater consideration in recent years. *The Young Card-Players* is closely related in composition to a small picture on copper in Paris (Musée du Louvre), the only substantial difference being the two grown-up figures standing behind. A contemporary copy or version combining features from both the painting in Paris and the present picture is in Worcester Art Museum, Mass. A connection with *L'intérieur d'une tabagie* (Paris, Musée du Louvre), dated 1643, has been proposed. This last is a large picture and a more ambitious composition.

The subject of card players, or related motifs, is associated with Caravaggio and his followers in Rome, but it is also found in the work of the *Bamboccianti*, a group of Dutch painters based in Rome that formed around Pieter van Laer (called Bamboccio) at the beginning of the seventeenth century and singled out for their depictions of 'low-life'. However, the social status of the figures in some of the paintings by Le Nain is not always easy to discern.

The artistic merits of *The Young Card-Players*, on the other hand, are not difficult to discern. The carefully drawn figures, the sharpness of the light entering the room from the left, the concentration on the game, the precise rendering of objects and clothes, and the enigmatic gesture of the boy peering round the door at the right are all noteworthy aspects. These features create an effect of heightened naturalism that not only intensifies the viewer's perception but charges the atmosphere with a mood of contemplation tinged with melancholy. It is a moment of calm that might at the next moment suddenly be shattered.

FROM BUCKINGHAM PALACE

REFERENCES: *Les frères Le Nain*, Paris, Grand Palais, 1978–9, No. 17; *Treasures from the Royal Collection*, The Queen's Gallery, Buckingham Palace, 1988, No. 44; P. Rosenberg, *Tout l'oeuvre peint des Le Nain*, Paris, 1993, No. 22.

9

REMBRANDT VAN RIJN

1606 – 1669

'The Shipbuilder and his Wife' is a painting of the greatest significance, both in terms of Rembrandt's development and the history of the Royal Collection. The artist painted relatively few double portraits, and of the other three in his oeuvre *Cornelis Claesz. Anslo in Conversation with a Woman* (Berlin-Dahlem, Gemäldegalerie) of 1641 is closest in composition and treatment.

The present painting dates from Rembrandt's early maturity, shortly after he moved from Leiden to base himself in Amsterdam, where *The Anatomy Lesson of Dr. Tulp* (The Hague, Mauritshuis) of 1632 helped to establish his reputation. In 'The Shipbuilder and his Wife' the artist has transformed the High Renaissance treatment of the double portrait, which had become somewhat staid in the hands of Rembrandt's immediate predecessors in Holland – such as Thomas de Keyser – into the Baroque idiom. The focus of the composition is the letter, which unites the actions of both figures. The strong diagonal created by the outstretched arms of Griet Jans, who enters the room from the right and interrupts her husband's thought process, is countered by the direction of the light issuing from the window on the left. There is a contrast between the urgency of the gestures and the more passive source of the illumination that highlights the facial features of the ageing couple and penetrates the inner recesses of the room. The flesh tones betray a more open, supple style of brushwork emerging in Rembrandt's work. Several layers of paint, for example, have been used to build up the surface to suggest the texture of wrinkled skin. The artist has in fact combined portraiture

Jan Rijcksen (1561–1637) and his Wife, Griet Jans ('The Shipbuilder and his Wife')

1633
Oil on canvas
114.3 × 168.9 cm
There is evidence that at an uncertain date the canvas was reduced along the upper edge. Signed and dated on the sheet of drawings lying on the edge of the table: *Rembrandt. f:/ 1633.*

with genre, creating for himself the opportunity to portray greater insight into character and thus to elevate portraiture to a level of higher psychological import. Increasingly, this was to become one of the outstanding aspects of Rembrandt's work in all media.

Jan Rijcksen was a successful master shipbuilder as the papers (possibly material for a treatise rather than a design for a vessel) on the table indicate. By the time of this painting Rijcksen was aged seventy and living at a prominent address in Amsterdam; he was one of the highest-rated taxpayers in the city. The painting may also be interpreted in the light of contemporary comment on marriage in the Dutch Republic. A treatise by Jacob Cats, *Houwelyck* (1625), for instance, refers to marriage as a working partnership.

'The Shipbuilder and his Wife' was George IV's most spectacular purchase in the field of Dutch painting. At the beginning of the nineteenth century, the picture belonged to the famous Dutch collector Jan Gildemeester, and it was subsequently acquired in 1811 by George IV in London for 5,000 guineas – a staggering sum of money for those days, and easily the highest price he paid for a painting. The picture was initially hung in the Blue Velvet Room (Fig. 8) in Carlton House, where George IV lived until he had the palace demolished in 1827.

FROM BUCKINGHAM PALACE

REFERENCES: White, 1982, No. 160; D. R. Smith, 'Rembrandt's Early Double Portraits and the Dutch Conversation Piece', *Art Bulletin*, LXIV (1982), pp. 269–81; J. Bruyn, et. al., *A Corpus of Rembrandt's Paintings*, ii, The Hague, Boston, London, 1986, No. A 77, pp. 367–77.

10

ANTHONY VAN DYCK

1599-1641

Born in Antwerp, Anthony Van Dyck was a pupil of Rubens. An early visit to London in 1620–1 during the reign of James I was short-lived, and the artist spent the next five or so years travelling extensively in Italy. These years were of the greatest significance for the development of Van Dyck's personal style, and some of his finest early works were undertaken in Genoa. He worked in Antwerp from 1627 until the winter of 1631–2, when he painted at The Hague. In April 1632 he was appointed court painter to Charles I and Henrietta Maria. Apart from a short period in Brussels in 1634–5 and brief visits in 1640–1 to Antwerp and Paris, Van Dyck remained in London, living at Blackfriars until his death. He was knighted in 1632 and received an annual salary from the King after 1633, in addition to separate payments for pictures. Special facilities were made at Blackfriars so that the King could visit the painter in his studio. His success as a painter of religious subjects and of portraits was also acknowledged in Antwerp, where in 1634 Van Dyck was elected honorary Dean of the Guild of St Luke – a position previously given only to Rubens.

On being appointed court painter to Charles I, Van Dyck proceeded in his portraits to immortalize the Stuart court and to transform the course of English painting. That the artist was working on the eve of the Civil War and at the height of his artistic powers has led to his paintings often being interpreted in a romantic vein, prompted by the onset of war, the disintegration of the court and the execution of the King in 1649. A picture that is especially poignant is *Cupid and Psyche*, which was painted *c.* 1639–40 and is the only mythological subject undertaken by Van Dyck while at the English court. It is an outstanding example of the tradition of painting *poesie*. As official painter, Van Dyck was responsible for producing definitive images of the King and his family, several of which are still in the Royal Collection.

Portrait of a Woman is a fine example of Van Dyck's

Portrait of a Woman

c. 1634–5
Oil on canvas
208.3 × 118.1 cm

full-length portraiture. The sheen of the drapery, the intricacy of the lace, the care lavished on coiffure and jewellery, and the creamy flesh tones indicate the quality of Van Dyck's painterly approach. The setting serves to remind the viewer that the artist was also a superb landscape artist. On the basis of the coiffure, the portrait has been dated 1634/5 and may have been painted in Brussels.

The iconography is of particular interest, and the artist seems to have introduced into portraiture the motif of a woman about to dip her hand into a fountain. He uses it, for example, on two other occasions, *Marchesa Caterina Durazzo, c.* 1625 (Genoa, Palazzo Reale), and *Lucy Percy, Countess of Carlisle, c.* 1640 (Petworth, Earl Egremont). Originating in antiquity the motif passes through the Renaissance into the seventeenth century. The fountain refers to purity or chastity, just as the vase is a metaphor for feminine beauty. The landscape setting suggests a garden that can be interpreted in the light of the medieval *hortus conclusus*, a further reference to chastity. However, because Cupid in this instance forms part of the fountain's design and a rose bush grows nearby, the scene implies that this is 'a garden of love in which the sitter appears as a love-inspiring yet chaste presence'. Similar compliments to women can be found in seventeenth-century poetry. Such motifs in the work of Sir Peter Lely were also used later by Reynolds and Gainsborough. Of these last two artists it is Gainsborough who shows a greater kinship with the present portrait.

The painting was acquired by Frederick, Prince of Wales, by 1747 and symbolizes the admiration for Van Dyck felt by later members of the Royal Family.

FROM WINDSOR CASTLE
REFERENCES: Millar, 1962, No. 154; Erik Larsen, *The Paintings of Anthony Van Dyck*, Freren, 1988, i. pp. 381–2 and ii. No. 960 p. 377; Zirca Zaremba Filipczak, 'Reflections on Motifs in Van Dyck's Portraits', in *Anthony Van Dyck*, National Gallery of Art, Washington, 1990, pp. 60–62.

11

SIMON VOUET

1590–1649

Diana

1637
Oil on canvas
102 × 141 cm
Signed and dated on the quiver
in the lower right hand corner:
Simon Vouet F. Paris 1637

Diana was the goddess of hunting. She is shown with her dogs and holds an arrow. A crescent moon adorns her hair. A quiver of arrows is in the lower right corner. The composition was originally oval and has been cut. Confirmation of this is provided by an engraving by Michel Dorigny, the artist's son-in-law, dated 1638. This evidence makes better sense of the internal rhythms of the painting, with the curve created by the reclining position of the goddess continued by the muzzles of the two dogs, which point in opposite directions. The extended arm serves to complete the circle. Dorigny's engraving also helps to clarify the background in so far as Diana is resting by a cleft of rocks, beyond which can be seen a more open landscape. He engraved two other oval compositions in 1638, both of mythological subjects, *Venus and Adonis* and *Mars and Venus*, and it is possible that they originally formed part of the same decorative scheme.

Vouet was appointed Premier Peintre du Roi to Louis XIII in 1627 after working for ten years in Rome, where in 1624 he had been elected President of the Accademia di San Luca. The artist's initial activity was in Italy, where he is recorded in Venice in 1613 before making his way to Rome. There and in Naples, Genoa, Modena and Bologna, he painted large-scale altarpieces. On returning to Paris he achieved great success, and his supremacy was only threatened when Poussin returned from Rome for two years in 1640. Although he continued to paint altarpieces in France, Vouet broadened his repertoire to include poetical, mythological and allegorical themes, which he often incorporated into extensive ceiling decorations. These are notable for their illusionism, which is dependent upon steep perspective, with the figures seen in direct relation to the room's architecture. His masterpiece in this respect was the decorative scheme for the Hôtel Seguier in Paris, now known only through engravings. Vouet's contribution to French painting was immensely important for its development in the mid-seventeenth century. Poussin was undoubtedly a greater painter, but Vouet was highly influential. This was mainly because of the wide terms of reference in his work, which amalgamated the influence of Caravaggio, Roman Baroque, Bolognese classicism and Venetian Renaissance painting. *Diana*, for instance, alludes to the Venetian tradition of Titian and Palma Vecchio, but at the same time refers back to the Mannerist works of Primaticcio and others undertaken for Francis I at Fontainebleau at the beginning of the sixteenth century.

The painting may have belonged to Charles I, but there is no documentary evidence to support this. The theorist André Felibien states that Vouet sent paintings to England, though he is not specific. Such a possibility, however, does seem likely, since the artist did execute an allegorical ceiling decoration entitled *Allegory of Peace between England and France* in celebration of the marriage of Charles I and Henrietta Maria, which took place in 1625. Even though the ceiling does not survive, it is known through an engraving dated 1639 recording that the decoration was carried out for Oatlands, a royal residence in Surrey used by Tudor and Stuart monarchs.

FROM HAMPTON COURT PALACE
REFERENCES: W. R. Crelly, *The Painting of Simon Vouet*, New Haven–London, 1962, pp. 115 and 166, No. 41; Lloyd, 1991, No. 30.

12

CLAUDE GELLEE, *called* LE LORRAIN

1600–1682

Harbour Scene at Sunset

1643
Oil on canvas
74 × 99 cm
Dated on the bale carried by the
man right of centre: *1643*

Harbour scenes at sunset with water gently lapping the shore occur frequently in Claude's paintings. Such themes do not always have a specifically identifiable subject but are sometimes pure landscapes evoking the beauty of the Italian coastline. Claude went to Rome from Nancy early in life (*c.* 1613) to become a pastry cook, but after taking employment with the landscape painter, Agostino Tassi, he emerged as a painter. Returning to France for a short visit (1625–7), he travelled back to Italy, where he remained for the rest of his life in Rome. Leading Roman families and members of the Papal Curia supported his work. Claude's highly influential treatment of landscape itself owed much to northern European artists established in Rome. More important still, the depictions are based on personal observations either retained in the mind or recorded in numerous drawings of Genoa, Naples, Città Vecchia and the Campagna to the south of Rome, which eventually became distilled into paintings soaked in atmosphere and charged with emotion.

For Claude's paintings are not only evocative of the landscape of Italy but of its ancient history. Neither Imperial nor Republican Rome interested Claude. Rather, it was the Golden Age in Virgil's *Aeneid* describing how Aeneas landed and founded Rome, or the *Georgics* with its emphasis on the pastoral. Virgil was the first poet to extol the beauty of Italy, and in European painting as a whole, for most observers, only Claude has emulated this achievement in paint.

Harbour Scene at Sunset, which was most probably acquired by Frederick, Prince of Wales, dates from the artist's middle years. There are, however, certain compositional connections with a drawing in Claude's *Liber Veritatis* (LV19), a record kept from 1635 by the artist himself of his finished paintings. LV19, in fact, relates to a picture dated 1637, and it is clear that the painter rethought the composition when he came to rework it in the following decade. The stylistic characteristics of *Harbour Scene at Sunset* are comparable with two much larger and more famous works by Claude dating from the 1640s, now in the National Gallery, London: *Seaport with the Embarkation of St Ursula* (1644) and *Seaport with the Embarkation of the Queen of Sheba* (1648) – this last inspiring J. M. W. Turner. These paintings have in common the deep ultramarine tones contrasting with the golden glow of the setting sun, the overall warmth of the colours and the firmer drawing that invests the figures with a greater feeling of corporeality. Of the buildings on the right only the monumental gateway next to the round tower is identifiable in so far as it is based on the Arcus Argentarium (Arch of the Silversmiths) dating from the third century AD at San Giorgio in Velabrio, Rome, although here it is seen in reverse and has been detached from the church.

Claude's paintings appealed particularly to collectors of the early nineteenth century, who responded to their style as much as to their subject matter. These aspects are still pleasing today, as in *Harbour Scene at Sunset* the eye regards the activities of the figures busying themselves loading and unloading ships, or simply idling the day away in the warm atmosphere and golden light of a summer's evening. Yet, it should be recalled that Claude was a very disciplined painter who conjured such scenes by means of careful organisation of space, subtle gradations of colour, delicate shifts in tone and an all-enveloping light. The final image may seem timeless, but there is movement everywhere as though in a state of flux. As one authority expressed it, Claude 'confined the infinity of nature within the rigid boundaries of classical composition'.

FROM WINDSOR CASTLE
REFERENCES: Lloyd, 1991, No. 42.

13

DAVID TENIERS THE YOUNGER

1610-1690

Peasants dancing
outside an Inn

c. 1645
Oil on canvas
105.3 × 205.1 cm

David Teniers the Younger was a prolific painter who specialized in peasant genre scenes of a type that had been pioneered in Flanders by Jan Brueghel the Elder, Frans Francken II and David Vinckeboons. His first marriage was in fact to the daughter of Jan Brueghel the Elder, Anne, but she died in 1656. The broad characterization of the figures is to some extent derived from Adriaen Brouwer, who served as an important link between the Flemish and Dutch schools. However, the squat proportions with large heads, short legs and big feet are instantly recognizable as being the work of Teniers. Not all the people in the present painting are peasants. The couple accompanied by their child and a dog in the left foreground are bourgeois types, as is the woman nearby being helped to her feet. Dress and coiffure suggest different social distinctions, and paintings of this sort often concealed meanings that have to be decoded in a broader social context. Teniers was an immensely varied painter who depicted a wide range of subjects – religious, allegorical, still life, flowers and interiors of galleries. His work runs the gamut of the social spectrum, and in this respect he anticipates Antoine Watteau, who was born in 1684 in Valenciennes, a Flemish town ceded to France only in 1678.

Peasants dancing outside an Inn is unusually large for a work by Teniers, but even though the demand for his pictures was so great that he was forced to use assistants, this painting is autograph throughout. The general layout of the composition, with buildings to the left, a tree positioned by a fence near the centre and a distant view to the right, is a well-established formula in Teniers's oeuvre. Indeed, the inn in the left half of the painting appears in several other pictures. It is the range of characterization, however, that holds the attention of the viewer: the bagpiper leaning against the tree, the man vomiting, the old man in the foreground leaning on his stick, the dancers, those sitting out the dance in various states of inebriation or indulging in various forms of

dalliance, the serving women glimpsed through the gate on the left or at the window above. It is a whole cast of characters on a crowded stage with all the movements carefully plotted but replete with varying emotions and changing rhythms dictated not just by the music but by the fluctuating fortunes of life. The figure helping the woman to her feet in the left half of the composition is not unworthy of Watteau, who admired Teniers. The importance of *Peasants dancing outside an Inn* is that it combines the artist's talent for genre, still life and landscape – these last being the principal passages on the extreme right of the painting.

Teniers was born in Antwerp. He was received as a Master of the Guild of Saint Luke in 1632–3, serving as Dean in 1645–6, and in 1663 he became a founder-member of the Académie Royale. From 1651 Teniers was court painter in Brussels to the Governor of the Spanish Netherlands, Archduke Leopold-Wilhelm, and his successor, Don Juan of Austria. Teniers then spent five years in England, apparently buying paintings in his capacity as an agent or as a dealer in his own right. He was a man of considerable wealth, purchasing a country estate in 1662 and being ennobled in 1680. His duties as court painter in Brussels involved advising Archduke Leopold-Wilhelm, who formed an art collection of the greatest significance. This was published in part by Teniers as *Le théâtre des peintures de David Teniers* (1660), the first illustrated catalogue to be printed. The artist himself made the painted copies on which the engravings were based, and some are in the Royal Collection.

The present painting was acquired in 1811 by George IV in London at the sale of the collection formed by Henry Hope. It was hung with other distinguished Dutch and Flemish pictures in the Bow Room of the Principal Floor of Carlton House and can be seen in the illustration to W. H. Pyne, *The History of the Royal Residences* (1819).

FROM BUCKINGHAM PALACE

REFERENCES: Lloyd, 1991, No. 49.

14

AELBERT CUYP

1620–1691

An Evening Landscape with Figures and Sheep

1655–60
Oil on canvas
101.6 × 153.6 cm
Signed lower right: *A cuÿp*

Cuyp was one of the most popular artists with British collectors during the late eighteenth and early nineteenth centuries. George IV shared this enthusiasm, and he acquired all seven of the paintings by Cuyp in the Royal Collection. *An Evening Landscape* is a supreme example of Cuyp's art and is one of the finest seventeenth-century Dutch paintings bought by the King. The picture has a most distinguished provenance, first being recorded towards the end of the eighteenth century in the collection of Johan van der Linden van Slingeland in Dordrecht, where Cuyp was born and lived for most of his life. This collection was sold in 1785 and included over twenty pictures by the artist, many of which subsequently passed indirectly into British collections. *An Evening Landscape* was next owned by Jan Gildemeester in Amsterdam, another important collection (it included No. 9 by Rembrandt in this exhibition). After the Gildemeester sale in 1800 the picture then went into the collection of the banker Sir Francis Baring that was purchased *en bloc* in 1814 on behalf of George IV. The quality of the picture is comparable with *River Landscape* (London, Dulwich Picture Gallery) and *River Landscape with Horseman and Peasants* (London, National Gallery), both of the same date. The result of the British enthusiasm for Cuyp, which continued into the Victorian period, was that Dutch collections were bereft of works by the artist.

The appeal of Cuyp's work lay in an appreciation both of the subject matter and of the artist's style. There is a feeling of calm and of peacefulness suggesting a well-ordered world that Cuyp's original patrons, as well as British aristocratic owners living on rural estates at a later date, saw as a visual representation of their own aspirations. The artist was a shrewd observer of the niceties of social status: forms of dress, groom of horse, style of riding, breed of dog, demeanour of servants. The social order depicted in these late, glorious landscapes by Cuyp is one of 'an order governed by land and hierarchy', and they represent 'a social process that transformed commercial oligarchs into landed gentry'. Interestingly, Cuyp himself was part of that process, for, although he was the son of a painter he married Cornelia Bosshman, the widow of a wealthy Regent, in 1650 and then held public office. His output as a painter declined during the 1650s, but those paintings that he did produce serve to underline his own social position and are a perfect reflection of his world.

Cuyp's early work is in the manner of Jan van Goyen and Salomon van Ruisdael, tending towards the monochromatic and replete with detailed observation. This early style was transformed (*c.* 1642) on seeing paintings in Utrecht by Jan Both, who had worked in Italy in the Campagna south of Rome. Cuyp's compositions thereafter became bathed in a warm golden light more evocative of Italy than of Holland. Furthermore, many of the buildings and the character of the landscape in these late paintings are based on Cuyp's experiences on a journey up the Rhine as far as Nijmegen and Kleve near the German border. Strictly speaking, they are not so much topographical views as imagined landscapes indicative of an alembicated existence. While the foreground of *An Evening Landscape* and the treatment of the trees are redolent of Cuyp's early work, the undulations in the landscape, the horizon disappearing into the hazy vaporous atmosphere and the tonal qualities are the signs of Cuyp's maturity. The varied handling of the paint, extending from the blades of grass in the foreground, where the yellow paint is spread like butter, to the smooth gradations in the sky, are the hallmarks of Cuyp at his very best.

FROM BUCKINGHAM PALACE

REFERENCES: White, 1982, No. 350; *Carlton House. The Past Glories of George IV's Palace*, The Queen's Gallery, Buckingham Palace, 1991, No. 44.

15

PIETER DE HOOCH

1629–1684

Pieter de Hooch was born in Rotterdam and died in Amsterdam, but he is most admired for the paintings he did in Delft, where he is recorded between 1652 and 1661. From these years date those works in the artist's mature style for which he is best known today. Most of these are either interiors, courtyards, or garden scenes depicting the everyday activities of a thriving middle-class society. Such subjects had not occurred in de Hooch's work until his move to Delft, and they also indicate a change of style characterized by a precise ordering of space and striking effects of light.

These new developments were most probably inspired by local artists working in Delft, like Carel Fabritius, Gerrit Houckgeest and Emmanuel de Witte, who were principally architectural painters interested in creating new illusionistic effects through a more scientific approach to perspective. The artist who brought this style to an unrivalled degree of perfection was de Hooch's slightly younger contemporary, Vermeer. Unlike Vermeer, however, whose paintings often have a moral message, de Hooch favoured more straightforward genre scenes, and to this extent his pictures provide a carefully observed, almost reflective, record of life in seventeenth-century Holland. The 1650s mark the highpoint in Delft's contribution to painting, but, though short-lived, it was one of the most important moments in the evolution of Dutch art.

There are two prominent topographical features in the background of *A Courtyard in Delft at Evening*. To the right of centre are two towers: the taller one is that of the Nieuwe Kerk, where William the Silent, the founder of the Dutch Republic, was buried; and the smaller one is that of the Stadthuis. These public buildings often occur in the backgrounds of other paintings by de Hooch, but the gabled house (or one very similar to it) is also repeated in other works of this period, such as *Two Women with a Child in a Courtyard* (Toledo, Museum of Art) and

A Courtyard in Delft at Evening: A Woman Spinning

c. 1656
Oil on canvas
69.2 × 53.4 cm
Signed lower right corner:
P. D. Hooch

A Woman and a Child in a Bleaching Ground (England, Private Collection). When de Hooch combines architectural features in this way, his purpose is to create an epitome of Delft, or a topographical framework in which his artistic imagination can thrive while observing the quiet routines of daily life.

What makes *A Courtyard in Delft at Evening* so effective as a painting is the treatment of light. The soft evening light, with shadows lengthening across the courtyard, is extraordinarily atmospheric. The seated figure is in shadow, whereas the standing figure is half in sunlight and half in shadow. De Hooch vividly captures the shifts in tone that changing light demands. Light during the day has a descriptive quality, but the suffused light of early evening has different properties and creates different effects. It is a mark of de Hooch's skill that his eye is no less diligent in depicting the brickwork, whitewash and tiles seen in this half-light. Indeed, the irregularity and random aspect of such features, suggesting the act of application, are in stark contrast with the tight, well-ordered composition as a whole, with its web of verticals, horizontals and diagonals enhanced by the silhouettes of the buildings. The two women, one with her back to the viewer, are firmly anchored within these spatial divisions and absorbed in their work. The nineteenth-century novelist George Eliot found Dutch genre paintings of this type deeply satisfying. 'I find a source of delicious sympathy in these faithful pictures of a homely existence, which has been the fate of so many more among my fellow immortals than a life of absolute indigence of tragic suffering or of world-stirring actions' (*Adam Bede*, 1859).

FROM BUCKINGHAM PALACE
REFERENCES: White, 1982, No. 84; Christopher Wright, *Dutch Painting in the Seventeenth Century: Images of a Golden Age in British Collections*, London, 1989, No. 82.

16

JAN STEEN

1625/6–1679

Jan Steen was well qualified to paint the interior of taverns since he was the son of a brewer and he himself leased a brewery during the 1650s. In 1672, towards the end of his life, he opened his own tavern in Leiden. The male figure laughing by the hearth on the left in the present painting is in all probability a self-portrait. Genre scenes dominate Steen's oeuvre, and the subjects often come into that category of picture that the eighteenth century tended to condemn on theoretical grounds and that the Victorians so heartily disapproved of on moral grounds. More recent critics prefer to use a comparison with Molière.

The early literature stresses the profligate nature of Steen's life, although there is no definite evidence to prove this, and the temptation to interpret his paintings on an autobiographical basis should be resisted. He may simply have been bohemian (the expression 'a Jan Steen household' is still used in Holland to describe an untidy or lively home), but he did attend Leiden University and was versed in Latin. His paintings are not always straightforward representations of everyday life, but they often illustrate proverbs and are overlaid with allegorical meaning, or even, as here, have political significance. The chandelier with a suspended bell (*belkroon*) in the centre of the room is decorated with a leafy branch, which denotes a special celebration. The clue to what exactly is being celebrated is the print on the back wall: it shows a man on a charging horse, an image associated with the Prince of Orange (the future William III), whose birthday was celebrated on 15 November (Prince's Day).

The painting amalgamates many of the best features of Steen's style – breadth of characterization and precise rendering of drapery and still-life objects. The composition is based on an inverted triangle, the apex of which is the flagon in the foreground, with the chair forming one side and the table the other, both leading back into the picture space. The figures are placed in the middle

Interior of a Tavern with Cardplayers and a Violin Player

c. 1665–8
Oil on canvas
81.9 × 69.2 cm
Signed lower left corner: *J Steen* (*JS* in monogram)

distance, with the violin player, though conversing with a young woman, set slightly apart from the rest of the company, as Degas was to do in some of his paintings of ballet rehearsals. Prominent on the table on the right is a dish of oysters (symbol of lasciviousness), and around it are grouped card-players. The female figure on the extreme right turns and faces the viewer, holding up an ace of diamonds. The knowing glance supported by the presence of the highly coiffured dog by the table suggests that the woman is a prostitute.

Steen was a prolific artist who painted about eight hundred pictures, only a small percentage of which are of religious subjects or portraits. Most of his compositions abound with energy, and it is only at the close of his career that a more elegiac mood (almost French in feeling) can be detected. Steen frequently used stock figures based on contemporary theatrical companies or groups of rhetoricians known as *rederijkers*. He was particularly good at portraying children, whose innocence served to point up the meaning of his paintings. Although he was closely associated with Leiden for most of his life, Steen was essentially peripatetic and lived for short periods in The Hague, Delft and Haarlem, but never in Amsterdam. His first teachers were equally diverse, Nikolaus Knüpfer in Utrecht, Adriaen van Ostade in Haarlem and Jan van Goyen, whose daughter he married, in The Hague. The paradoxical elements of his style – broad characterization contrasted with a love of detail – reveal at one moment an allegiance to Hals and at another to Frans van Mieris the Elder or Gerrit Dou (the leading *fijnschilders* of Leiden). Because so many of Steen's pictures are interiors, it can be unexpected when he introduces landscape elements into his paintings, just as his jubilant use of colour is sometimes surprising.

Interior of a Tavern with Cardplayers and a Violin Player was acquired by George IV.

FROM BUCKINGHAM PALACE
REFERENCES: White, 1982, No. 191; Lloyd, 1991, No. 55.

17

JOHN RILEY

1646−1691

Bridget Holmes

1686
Oil on canvas
225.4 × 148.6 cm
Signed: *I. R. PI.t* (lower right)
and inscribed *BRIDGET.*
HOLMES. | ET Aa SUAE: 96.
A:D: 1686 (lower left).

John Riley was appointed Principal Painter to William III and Mary II in succession to Antonio Verrio (1639−1707) after the Glorious Revolution in 1688. He held the post jointly with the more famous artist Sir Godfrey Kneller (1646−1729), who ultimately came to dominate painting in Britain during the last quarter of the seventeenth century, as the Stuart dynasty drew to a close. Riley's career in royal circles had begun *c.* 1680 inauspiciously with a portrait of Charles II, of which the King is reported to have remarked, 'Is this like me? Oddsfish then I'm an ugly fellow'. This may not, however, have been a comment on Riley's skills so much as on the directness of his approach to portraiture. His drawing can appear faulty or wooden, and there is sometimes an uncertainty in the structure of his compositions, perhaps in response to European influences purveyed by such major painters as Van Dyck, Sir Peter Lely or Kneller. Nonetheless, Riley holds a significant position in the development of the native school of British portrait painting. There is, in fact, a line of direct descent that leads from Riley through Jonathan Richardson the Elder to Thomas Hudson, who was the first master of Sir Joshua Reynolds. *Bridget Holmes* is a memorable example of a full-length portrait by the artist. The warm tones, silvery lighting effects and softness of the brushwork reveal Riley's true, if limited, qualities.

The candour that the painter demonstrated in his portrait of Charles II has in this case been turned to his advantage. Bridget Holmes was a 'Necessary Woman' at the Court and is shown brandishing the brush that is the attribute of her duties. She lived to be one hundred years of age, and she has been depicted here four years before her death in a playful mood with a Page of the Backstairs, possibly at Windsor Castle.

It was rare in the seventeenth century, even less so in subsequent centuries, for domestic servants to be the subject of portraits. There are, however, at least two other examples in Riley's oeuvre: *A Scullion* (Oxford, Christ Church) and *Katherine Elliot*, painted jointly with J. B. Closterman (Royal Collection). As one writer has expressed it, 'Riley was most at home below stairs'. For *Bridget Holmes* Riley has used the trappings of the more formal portraiture that he might have been expected to produce in his role as Principal Painter. These include the monumentality of the figure, the curtain and the antique vase, which is based on a print of 1582 made by Cherubino Alberti after a fresco by Polidoro Caravaggio (*c.* 1495−1543) on the façade of the Palazzo Milesi in Rome. It is possible that some satirical or moral connotation was intended, as in the case of such contemporary Dutch painters as Nicolaes Maes, but this would run counter to Riley's somewhat modest and unpretentious approach to portrait painting. Yet this image of Bridget Holmes anticipates both William Hogarth and Reynolds in its treatment of subject and visual allusions.

FROM WINDSOR CASTLE

REFERENCES: Millar, 1963, No. 330: T. Clifford, 'Polidoro and English Design', *Connoisseur*, CXCII (1976), pp. 284−5: J. Douglas Stewart, *Sir Godfrey Kneller and the English Baroque Portrait* (Oxford, 1983), p. 32; Lloyd, 1991, No. 33.

BRIDGET. HOLMES
ETA⁴ SUÆ: 96 A:D: 1686

18

JOHN WOOTTON

c.1682–1764

A View of Henley-on-Thames from the East

c. 1742–1743
Oil on canvas
101 × 156.2 cm

A*View of Henley-on-Thames* was painted in the grounds of Park Place, a country house acquired by Frederick, Prince of Wales, *c.*1738 from Lord and Lady Archibald Hamilton. There are two related paintings of similar dimensions by Wootton in the Royal Collection: *A Distant View of Henley-on-Thames* is again painted in the grounds of Park Place but from further away, with the town partially obscured by a hill; the other is a view of Park Place itself, seen from the opposite direction from the other side of the river in the fields near Henley-on-Thames. These pictures were probably painted originally to be hung as a group possibly in Park Place. According to Horace Walpole, they were executed for Lady Archibald Hamilton and either presented to or purchased by Frederick, Prince of Wales.

Henley-on-Thames is located about halfway between London and Oxford. Park Place was built by Lord Archibald Hamilton (1673–1754) in 1719, but the house no longer survives. Lady Archibald Hamilton (died 1752) was a member of the Household attending Frederick, Prince of Wales, and his wife, Augusta, Princess of Wales. Hamilton was appointed Keeper of the Privy Purse in 1736, then Lady of the Bedchamber and Mistress of the Robes. After Park Place was acquired by the Prince of Wales, it is apparent that Lord and Lady Hamilton continued to live on the estate. There was, however, a political dimension to the acquisition of Park Place, since in 1737 the Prince of Wales had quarrelled with his father, George II, and was banished from the court at St James's Palace. A later owner of Park Place, Field Marshal Henry Seymour Conway, made alterations to the house and embellished it in the picturesque style, moving his cousin Horace Walpole to describe it as 'one of the most charming places in England where "Pan & the Sylvan Deities" seem to have made it their favourite residence, and Father Thames ennobles it by his fair stream'.

A View of Henley-on-Thames depicts the end of a hunt. The Prince of Wales is on horseback in the left foreground. He wears the Order of the Garter and is surrounded by other horsemen. On the right is a group of falconers, grooms with dogs and farm labourers. Dividing these two groups is a carriage drawn by six horses, greeting the huntsmen. The royal coat of arms is emblazoned on the carriage door, and the Prince of Wales's feathers can also be made out. In the carriage are Augusta, Princess of Wales (or conceivably Lady Archibald Hamilton), and four royal children: the Princes, George (later George III) and Edward, and the Princesses, Augusta and Elizabeth. The scene is bathed in a warm evening light, and there are long cast shadows.

John Wootton was a painter of landscapes, sporting pictures and military pieces. He made a most important contribution to the development of landscape and military painting, enjoying the widespread patronage of leading members of the aristocracy and of the Royal Family. Although the views of Henley-on-Thames by Wootton are topographically accurate, they are carefully composed and imbued with atmosphere. The figures are admittedly given prominence in the foreground, but their anecdotal interest is subservient to the expansive view spread out behind them. The influence of Claude Lorrain is apparent.

On a different level Wootton's paintings of Henley-on-Thames are instructive from the point of view of how the English countryside looked in the early eighteenth century: the division of the fields, extent of forestation, relationship of the town to the surrounding landscape, use of the river and methods of farming.

FROM WINDSOR CASTLE
REFERENCES: Millar, 1963, No. 549: *The Royal Collection: Paintings from Windsor Castle*, Cardiff, National Museum of Wales, 1991, No. 54.

19

CANALETTO

1697–1768

The view is of the south end of the Grand Canal, close to where it emerges into the Bacino di San Marco, the hub of Venice. Prominent on the right is the church of Santa Maria della Salute, with the Seminario adjoining it and the top of the Punta della Dogana (Custom's House) visible beyond. On the left are numerous palaces once inhabited by noble families, including those of Tiepolo, Treves dei Bonfili and Giustiniani. The top of the Campanile in the Piazza di San Marco rises above the roofs of these palaces, as does the campanile of the church of San Moisé on the far left. Further along the canal on the left, the Palazzo Ducale (Doge's Palace) can be seen with the column of San Marco topped by the winged lion, the symbol of St Mark and thus of Venice. Stretching into the distance beyond the Prisons next to the Palazzo Ducale is the Riva degli Schiavoni, in front of which several vessels and craft can be seen in the Bacino. The unfinished façade of the church of S. Maria della Visitazione (the Pietà) – which is so closely associated with the music of Antonio Vivaldi, who composed there from 1703 until his death in 1741 – is also visible in this range of buildings.

The church of S. Maria della Salute is one of the finest Baroque buildings in Venice. It was designed by Baldassare Longhena as a thanksgiving for the city's deliverance from the terrible plague of 1630. Begun in 1631, it was not completed until 1681, lasting for almost the whole of the architect's working life.

The view occurs often in Canaletto's oeuvre, the earliest treatment of the theme being the picture in Dresden dating from *c.*1726. An example from the following decade is in the Royal Collection and forms part of a series of views of the Grand Canal on a smaller scale that was painted for Consul Joseph Smith and engraved by Antonio Visentini for the volume entitled *Prospectus Magni Canalis Venetiarum* (1735). The present painting is on an unusually large scale for Canaletto and may be the

Venice:
The Grand Canal
with S. Maria
della Salute
looking towards the
Bacino di San Marco

1744
Oil on canvas
126 × 202.6 cm
Signed and dated on the moored
barge in the centre foreground:
A Canal 1744 (AC in ligature)

artist's last picture of the subject. No precise version of the composition is known.

Canaletto, whose real name was Antonio Canal, is the most famous of the view painters of Venice who developed the tradition of Luca Carlevarijs. Trained as a painter of stage scenery by his father in Rome, the early views of Venice done in the 1720s are characterized by strong contrasts in colour, dynamic handling of paint and a greater feeling for atmosphere. Gradually, as his work became popular – particularly with visitors on the Grand Tour – Canaletto's style became more rigid and the execution more mechanical, even though he hardly ever failed to capture the magical effect of the light in Venice with the sun playing on the water. The topographical emphasis, which is not always strictly accurate, is offset by the constantly moving reflections, the sudden shifts into shadow and by the anecdotal details recording everyday life in the city. On the right, for example, figures on the steps of S. Maria della Salute enliven the scene, quite apart from the activity on the Grand Canal. Although Canaletto's name is so inextricably linked with Venice, he depicted a series of views of Rome in 1742, and he also painted in London (between 1746 and 1755). Furthermore, he made frequent journeys to Padua, travelling up the Brenta Canal, which seemed to have a liberating effect and resulted in several *capricci*, or imaginative views.

The Royal Collection has the greatest – certainly the most comprehensive – holding of paintings by Canaletto in the world; there are nearly fifty pictures by the artist. This is due to the purchase by the young George III in 1762 of the collection formed by Consul Smith (*c.* 1674–1770), an English merchant-banker and collector who resided in Venice from *c.*1700 and was Canaletto's main patron.

FROM WINDSOR CASTLE
REFERENCES: Levey, 1991, No. 407.

20

JOSEPH NICKOLLS

1726–1755

The artist has depicted the east end of the Mall looking towards Westminster Abbey, visible through the trees. On the left in the background is a glimpse of Horse Guards with a company of soldiers marching beneath the walls enclosing the garden of No. 10 Downing Street, the official residence of the Prime Minister.

St James's Park was opened to the public by Charles II shortly after the Restoration in 1660, when a canal was cut (seen in the middle distance of the present painting), avenues of trees planted and a raised area boarded in for playing the game of pall mall (an early form of croquet), which was introduced to London by Charles I on the site of the street that today is called Pall Mall. St James's Park was divided into three main avenues, or walks, of which the most important was the Mall. In addition to the canal there was a pond.

From the start St James's Park proved to be popular for promenading in the French style, and even though the game of pall mall had ceased to be played there by the end of the seventeenth century, the park continued to be frequented by courtiers and fashionable people. The proximity to St James's Palace, where the court was based, made the Mall the height of fashion during the eighteenth century. The Frenchman César de Saussure visited London in 1725 and recorded that 'Society comes to walk here on fine, warm days, from seven to ten in the evening, and in winter from one to three o'clock ... the park is so crowded at times that you cannot help touching your neighbour. Some people come to see, some to be seen, and others to seek their fortunes; for many priestesses of Venus are abroad ... all on the look-out for adventures'.

Nickolls depicts a cross-section of London society with the more sophisticated elements under the trees and others, including milkmaids, clergymen, sailors, soldiers (from Highland and Hanoverian regiments), Orientals and a mother breast-feeding, in the foreground. Even royalty could be seen on such occasions. The artist has

St James's Park and The Mall

c. 1745
Oil on canvas
104.1 × 138.4 cm

portrayed George II on the left, seen from the back wearing the blue riband of the Order of the Garter, while his son, Frederick, Prince of Wales, whom he detested, is more prominently placed just to the right of centre, accompanied by a man identified as the first Duke of Newcastle (1695–1768), an influential political figure of Whig persuasion. The architect John Gwynn wrote in 1766: 'The Mall in a summer's evening was formerly one of the highest entertainments that can well be conceived, it was here that the people at a respectable distance could behold to advantage some of the greatest personages and most beautiful objects in the kingdom, and the order and decorum in which it was kept at that time, was sufficient to deter the meaner part of the people from intruding into a place which seemed by no means suited to persons of their appearance.'

Towards the end of the eighteenth century, the formal layout of the park was landscaped by Lancelot 'Capability' Brown and the canal transformed into a lake. The Mall itself did not become a triumphal ceremonial route leading from Admiralty Arch to Buckingham Palace until the beginning of the twentieth century.

Numerous depictions of St James's Park and the Mall are known, from seventeenth-century topographical prints to mid- to late-eighteenth-century pictures and watercolours by British and French artists, several emulating the French tradition of the *fête galante*.

Joseph Nickolls was best known as an engraver, and this painting is reasonably attributed to him on the basis of his signed pictures, *The Fountain in the Middle Temple* of 1738 (London, The Honourable Society of the Middle Temple) and *A View of Charing Cross and Northumberland House* of 1746 (London, The National Westminster Bank Collection).

FROM BUCKINGHAM PALACE

REFERENCES: Millar, 1963, No. 617; M. Girouard, *Cities and People: A Social and Architectural History*, New Haven and London, 1985, p. 186; *Manners and Morals Hogarth and British Painting 1700–1760*, The Tate Gallery, London, 1987, No. 114; Celina Fox, *Londoners*, London, 1987, pp. 79–86.

21

WILLIAM HOGARTH

1697–1764

The portrait was presumably a personal commission from the actor David Garrick. It was reported to be in progress in 1757: 'Hogarth has got again into Portraits; and has his hands full of business, and at an high price. He has almost finished a most noble one of our sprightly friend David Garrick and his Wife: they are a fine contrast. David is sitting at a table, smilingly thoughtful over an epilogue ... his head supported by his writing hand; and Madam is archly enough stealing away his pen unseen behind. It is not so much fancy as to be affected or ridiculous and yet enough to raise it from the formal inanity of a mere Portrait' (letter of John Hoadly to Joseph Warton on 21 April 1757).

Even though Garrick paid the artist in 1763, the painting was still in the artist's studio on his death a year later. Tradition has it that a difference of opinion arose between Hogarth and Garrick (a notoriously proud and vain man) over the likeness, and it is apparent that the artist did have some difficulty with the eyes, where there are signs of erasure, particularly to the left eye. The X-ray evidence reveals that Hogarth had more profound difficulties with the composition. The background was originally a domestic interior with a bookcase and mirror, but these seem to have been overpainted and the figure of Garrick's wife altered. It may be that these parts of the canvas were unresolved when the artist received payment in 1763 and that, accordingly, Hogarth simplified the design to finish it more hastily. The composition is based on a pyramid, but the use of diagonals both enlivens the painting and fuses the two figures together without making the delicate balletic gestures and sense of movement appear to be forced. It is a superbly orchestrated rococo composition, the liveliness of which is enhanced by the design of the chair and the decorative aspects of the clothes. The pose of Garrick's wife in this respect is especially appropriate since she was a dancer.

As so often in Hogarth's work, reference is made to an earlier iconographical tradition, namely the subject of a

David Garrick with his Wife Eva-Maria Veigel, 'La Violette' or 'Violetti' (1725–1822)

c. 1757
Oil on canvas
133.3 × 104.1 cm
Signed: [W] *Hogarth*

genius inspired by a muse in classical art or the angel dictating the gospel to St Matthew in religious art. Yet on this occasion Hogarth indulges in role reversal, since Garrick's wife is playfully distracting her husband. The subject and composition make an interesting comparison with *The Shipbuilder and his Wife* by Rembrandt (see No. 9), but the real precedents lie in French painting: *The Letter-Writer* by Philippe Mercier and *Colley Cibber and his Daughter* (1738) by J. B. van Loo. The theme is continued after Hogarth by J. L. David in *Antoine-Laurent Lavoisier and his Wife*, dating from 1788 (New York, Metropolitan Museum).

The portrait is replete with personal references. Garrick was arguably the most versatile actor of the eighteenth century, responsible for a radical change in the style of acting and particularly noted for his performances in the tragedies and histories of Shakespeare. The political philosopher Edmund Burke remarked that Garrick 'raised the character of his profession to the rank of a liberal art'. His greatest performance was perhaps as the King in *Richard III*, first given in 1741, which inspired Hogarth's large painting now in Liverpool (Walker Art Gallery). The books on the table in the present portrait include a copy of Shakespeare's plays, but in front of Garrick is a draft of *The Prologue to Taste*, a comedy by Samuel Foote first performed in 1752.

The actor was depicted on numerous occasions by the greatest British artists of his time, but few are as private or as affectionate as Hogarth's image. Garrick married Eva-Maria Veigel in 1749. The portrait was presented to her by Hogarth's widow, the daughter of Sir James Thornhill, after the artist's death and remained in her possession until her own death. Soon afterwards it was acquired by George IV.

FROM WINDSOR CASTLE
REFERENCES: Millar, 1963, No. 560; *Carlton House: The Past Glories of George IV's Palace*, The Queen's Gallery, Buckingham Palace, 1991, No. 53.

22

JEAN-BAPTIST GREUZE

1725–1805

Silence!

1759
Oil on canvas
62.5 × 50.8 cm

The painting was exhibited in the Paris Salon of 1759 with the title, *Un tableau représentant le Repos, caracterisé par une Femme qui impose silence à son fils, en lui montrant ses autres enfants qui dorment.* It was lent on that occasion by one of Greuze's leading patrons, Jean de Jullienne (1686–1766), who was the close friend, leading collector and promoter of Antoine Watteau. The picture is a highly characteristic example of Greuze's art, although it did not receive overwhelming praise from the critics.

Born in Burgundy near Chalon-sur-Sâone, Greuze began to paint in Lyon with Charles Grandon but seems to have developed his style without undue allegiance to one particular painter. By 1755 he had moved to Paris but was not immediately successful at the Académie and so left for Italy, where he spent two years. The visit to Italy proved to be instructive, but Greuze's true style began during the 1760s with numerous genre scenes (often set in rustic contexts) and several ambitious historical paintings. A leading supporter was the influential critic Denis Diderot, but Greuze was ultimately accepted by the Académie in 1769 in the low category of a genre painter and not as a history painter, which may have been intended as a deliberate insult. During the 1770s Greuze increased his output as a genre painter, often interpreting religious themes, such as the Prodigal Son. By the end of the century, however, the political situation in France had changed, and painters of a more radical persuasion, like Jacques-Louis David, had emerged.

The paintings that Greuze produced for most of his career are imbued with *sensibilité*. The choice of subjects, the attitudes and expressions of his figures and the contrived poses amounted to a public display of feelings that had been suppressed in France at the turn of the seventeenth and eighteenth centuries. The origins of his art lie predominantly in seventeenth-century Dutch painting, but he also shows a knowledge of Flemish painting of the same period and was not unmoved by the works of Poussin. The appeal of such pictures by Greuze as *L'Accordée de Village*, dating from 1761 (Paris, Musée du Louvre), was immense, but the moralizing tone of so many of his paintings can seem overbearing. As one writer has put it, 'Greuze made the naive mistake, from which no amount of special pleading will excuse him, of supposing that a moving anecdote will make a moving work of art'. Though a powerful draughtsman, some of Greuze's allegorical paintings, usually of single female figures, verge towards the sentimental or border on titillation.

Silence! depicts a young mother imploring her dishevelled son to cease blowing his toy trumpet while her other younger children are sleeping. It seems that the broken drum, suspended from the back of the chair on the right, has also received his attentions. A painting of approximately the same dimensions, similar in setting and characterization entitled *L'enfant gâté* (St Petersburg, Hermitage Museum) and exhibited in the Salon of 1765, may have been intended as a pendant in so far as it portrays an indulgent mother in contrast with the reproving mother shown in the present picture. There are a number of preparatory drawings for *Silence!* The composition is apparently inspired by a painting by Nicolaes Maes, *La tricoteuse endormie*, which Greuze might have known through an engraving. The themes depicted in these and similar paintings by Greuze reflect the attitudes in eighteenth-century France to motherhood and the upbringing of children as promulgated in contemporary literature and drama. Through engravings Greuze's compositions achieved considerable fame, and their influence can be seen in nineteenth-century British art.

Silence! was acquired by George IV in 1817.

FROM BUCKINGHAM PALACE

REFERENCES: Anita Brookner, *Greuze*, London, 1972, pp. 60, 98 and 100; Edgar Munhall, *Jean-Baptiste Greuze 1725–1805*, Hartford, Wadsworth Atheneum, 1976, No. 23; *Carlton House, The Past Glories of George IV's Palace*, The Queen's Gallery, Buckingham Palace, 1991, No. 182.

23

THOMAS GAINSBOROUGH

1727–1788

James Quin
(1693–1766)

1763
Oil on canvas
64.8 × 50.8 cm

Gainsborough exhibited a full-length portrait of the actor James Quin at the Society of Arts in 1763. The portrait is now in the National Gallery of Ireland in Dublin. The figure is seated in a chair with the body seen in three-quarters profile to the right, the head turned to left facing out of the composition. The lips are parted as though in conversation with a closed book of plays in one hand (the thumb is inserted to mark the page) and the other gesturing. It is an animated image ultimately derived by the artist from the example of Van Dyck, as in such works as *Cardinal Bentivoglio*, dating from 1622/3 (Florence, Palazzo Pitti), though reversed. It was perhaps also partly inspired by the etching, *Portrait of Lord Simon Lovat* (1746) by William Hogarth. The expression on Quin's face is comparable with that of an apotheosis in religious depictions, but Gainsborough's intention was more realistic, namely to make the viewer aware of a figure outside the pictorial composition. As one writer observed, it was at this phase of Gainsborough's development that he 'reached the finest balance of observed truth and imagination'. A fellow artist, Ozias Humphrey, described the portrait as being of 'uncommon force and vigour, with a truth and animation beyond Mr. Gainsborough's usual performance'.

The painting in the Royal Collection has almost certainly been cut from a larger canvas, and it may be that Gainsborough originally intended the portrait of Quin to be a half-length following the examples of both Thomas Hudson and Hogarth (London, Tate Gallery). This study of Quin's head was clearly painted from life: it has been deftly brushed on to the canvas, and the image possesses an immediacy and spontaneity that are characteristic of Gainsborough's portraits. The artist retains this position for the head in the final portrait in Dublin, and indeed, the type was used again by Thomas King for the relief on the monument to Quin in the Abbey at Bath.

Gainsborough may have known Quin slightly in London on his first arrival there during the 1740s, but in fact, he painted his portrait in Bath, to which the actor retired and where the painter worked successfully from 1760–74. It is clear that Quin spent a considerable amount of time with the painter in Bath and they shared a similar bawdy sense of humour and love of drink. Quin was born in Dublin but came to London in 1715, acting at Lincoln's Inn Fields Theatre, Covent Garden and Drury Lane until his retirement in 1751. He was primarily a Shakespearean actor, playing nearly all the tragic leads, as well as Falstaff, in which he was said to have been particularly good. Quin's acting was in the tradition of Thomas Betterton – stilted, declamatory and overdressed. Richard Cumberland describes Quin's acting style as follows: 'With very little variation of cadence, and in a deep full tone, accompanied by a sawing kind of action, which had more of the senate than the stage in it, he rolled out his heroics with an air of dignified indifference.' This did not compare well with Garrick's more natural style, although both men admired one another. 'If the young fellow is right,' Quin once said of Garrick, 'I and the rest of the players have been all wrong.' Horace Walpole preferred Quin's style to Garrick's. Lacking a formal education, Quin was vain, obstinate and quick-tempered (he killed two fellow actors in arguments) but nonetheless generous and warm-hearted. The novelist Tobias Smollett says of Quin in his novel *Humphrey Clinker* (not published until 1771) that his 'wit was apt to degenerate into extreme coarseness and manner into extreme arrogance'. When Quin was reluctant to have his portrait painted Gainsborough apparently remarked, 'If you will let me take your likeness, I shall live for ever, and this persuaded him to sit'. The actor left the artist £50 in his will. The portrait remained in the artist's studio at his death and is only first recorded in the Royal Collection during the reign of Queen Victoria. In January 1749 Quin rehearsed the children of Frederick, Prince of Wales, in a performance of *Cato* and claimed to have given the young George III lessons in elocution.

FROM BUCKINGHAM PALACE

REFERENCES: Millar, 1963, No. 803; *Treasures from the Royal Collection*, The Queen's Gallery, Buckingham Palace, 1988, No. 32.

24

JOHANN ZOFFANY

1733–1810

John Cuff
(c. 1708–1777)

1772
Oil on canvas
89.5 × 69.2 cm
Signed and dated: *Zoffany
pinx/1772*

The artist was born near Frankfurt, and he quickly rose to be court painter at Regensburg (Prince von Thurn und Taxis) and Trier (Prince Archbishop and Elector of Trier). Sometime during 1760 he moved to London, where he had difficulty at first in establishing himself. The actor David Garrick (see No. 21) was one of his earliest patrons, and through him the artist made his name as a painter of theatrical scenes. It was, however, another early patron, Lord Bute, who brought Zoffany to the attention of his most significant patrons, George III and Queen Charlotte, for whom he painted some of his best known pictures – *Queen Charlotte with her two eldest Sons*, dating from *c.* 1765, and *The Tribuna of the Uffizi*, exhibited in 1780. At George III's insistence Zoffany was nominated as a member of the Royal Academy in 1769, from which stemmed his picture of *The Academicians of the Royal Academy*, exhibited in 1772. In that same year Zoffany left for Italy, returning in 1779 after receiving honours in Florence, Bologna, Cortona and Parma. On his return he painted *The Sharp Family* (on loan to the National Portrait Gallery) for William Sharp, surgeon to George III, but in an increasingly desperate search for patrons he left in 1783 for India, where he remained painting portraits of members of the British community until 1789. Further short visits to Germany and India during the 1790s did little to alleviate his reduced circumstances or to forestall his declining powers as an artist. At his best Zoffany was a leading exponent of the family conversation piece, combining informal compositions with a carefully crafted technique. The precision of his drawing, richness of colouring, crispness of paint and ability to capture a likeness were his chief strengths, conflating German and English artistic traditions.

John Cuff displays all the best qualities of Zoffany's art. The painting was in all probability executed for George III, and it was exhibited at the Royal Academy in 1772.

On that occasion, however, it was criticized rather perversely by Horace Walpole as 'Extremely natural, but the characters too common nature, and the chiaroscuro destroyed by his [Zoffany's] servility in imitating the reflexions of the glasses'. In fact, the aspects that Walpole disliked most are exactly those that make it interesting today, for painted images of craftsmen in a work setting at this date are rare. It was not unusual for inventors and scientific instrument makers to be painted as subjects of formal portraiture displaying their attributes or inventions but not often while at work.

John Cuff was an optician whose shop was 'at the sign of the Reflecting Microscope, exactly against Sergeants' Inn Gate, Fleet St'. He was Master of the Spectacle Makers Company in 1748 and involved with the development of microscopes, which he made for George III, who was fascinated by scientific instruments, and Queen Charlotte. The identification of the seated figure as John Cuff goes back to the eighteenth century, but it has been challenged, even though the sitter was receiving payments from the King in 1770 and 1771 and could therefore still have been a subject for royal portraiture.

The canvas has been added to by the artist along the lower edge, and changes are visible in the rendering of the window, the bench, the figure of the assistant and the lower half of Cuff's body. The meticulous accumulation of detail, the animated expressions and the sharpness of the light are important stylistic features in a painting that fuses portraiture with genre and is at the same time an exercise in still life.

FROM WINDSOR CASTLE

REFERENCES: Millar, 1969, No. 1209; Mary Webster, *Johann Zoffany 1733–1810*, National Portrait Gallery, 1976, No. 71; Celina Fox, *Londoners*, London, 1987, pp. 111 and 266; *Treasures from the Royal Collection*, The Queen's Gallery, Buckingham Palace, 1988, No. 33.

25

JOHN SINGLETON COPLEY

1738—1815

The Three Youngest Daughters of George III

1785
Oil on canvas
265.5 × 186 cm
Signed and dated: *J. S. Copley
1785* and on the cart *PA*
(in monogram)

The artist was born in Boston of Irish parents and quickly established himself as the foremost painter of portraits in the American colonies. His style is marked by a directness and sincerity of approach due to the fact that he was essentially self-taught. Copley sent several works to the Royal Academy from 1760 until 1767 that were well received. This encouraged him to leave Boston to absorb at source the lessons offered by the European tradition. Accordingly, in 1774–5 he travelled in Italy, Germany and the Netherlands before settling in London. There he was advised by Benjamin West, a fellow American who in 1772 had become Historical Painter to George III and in 1792 was to succeed Sir Joshua Reynolds as the second President of the Royal Academy. Copley was elected a member of the Royal Academy in 1779, one year after he painted his most famous picture, *Brook Watson and the Shark* (Washington D.C., National Gallery of Art, and Boston, Museum of Fine Arts). He gained further renown through his depictions of contemporary historical scenes, for example, *The Death of Chatham, The Death of Major Pierson, The Repulse of the Floating Batteries at Gibraltar.*

The commission to paint *The Three Youngest Daughters of George III* for the King and Queen was apparently obtained by West. The painter has depicted nine-year-old Princess Mary (1776–1817), on the left striking a tambourine to amuse her four-year-old sister, Princess Amelia (1783–1810), seated in the carriage, behind whom is Princess Sophia (1777–1848), eight years old. The figures are playing beneath an arbour with vines. Sunflowers can be seen on the left and other flowers in the lower right corner. Above, two parrots pick at bunches of grapes as though echoing the playful activities of the children and the dogs in the lower half of the composition. The figures are arranged in the shape of an inverted triangle, the apex of which is the seated spaniel. Visible in the distance is a view of Windsor Castle below a summer sky seen towards evening.

Copley was a slow worker and prepared his compositions with numerous drawings. According to the artist C. R. Leslie, 'the children, the dogs, and the parrots became equally wearied. The persons who were obliged to attend them while sitting complained to the Queen; the Queen complained to the King; and the King to Mr West ... Mr West satisfied His Majesty that Mr Copley must be allowed to proceed in his own way, and that any attempt to hurry him might be injurious to the picture, which would be a very fine one when done'. It is true that the sense of movement, internal rhythms and confident handling of paint on this large work could only have been achieved as a result of the care with which Copley plotted the composition. The painting has been referred to as a rococo conversation piece and described as 'agreeably unEnglish, since the children conduct themselves in a manner which, though not uncommon with children, is more lively than most British parents liked to have perpetuated in a picture'. The artist John Hoppner wrote, 'Why, you have plucked up harmony by the roots and planted confusion in its stead'. Copley seems to be illustrating the theories propounded by philosophers of the Enlightenment.

The Three Youngest Daughters of George III holds an important position in the rich tradition of painting royal children. Van Dyck, Zoffany and Gainsborough were important forerunners, while West, Lawrence, Hoppner and Beechey added to the tradition later. To a certain extent Copley's emphasis on nature in the foreground recalls the decorative schemes painted by the childrens' elder sister, Princess Elizabeth, in the Cross Gallery in Frogmore House, where there is also a whole room of floral paintings (garlands, swags and bouquets) by Mary Moser (1744–1819), both projects dating from the 1790s.

FROM WINDSOR CASTLE
REFERENCES: Millar, 1969, No. 712; Andrew Wilton, *The Swagger Portrait: Grand Manner Portraiture in Britain from Van Dyck to Augustus John 1630–1930*, Tate Gallery, London, 1992, No. 44.

26

GEORGE STUBBS

1724—1806

There is a large group of paintings by Stubbs in the Royal Collection; all were almost certainly commissioned by George IV or else acquired by him. With only a single exception these paintings date from the 1790s, and several of them were framed identically. A bill dated 14 February 1793 for frames made by Thomas Allwood states: 'To Carving & Gilding eight Picture frames of half length size for Sundry Pictures painted by Mr. Stubbs, all of one pattern'. The present painting is surrounded by one of Allwood's frames.

Stubbs is best known as a painter of animals, particularly horses. His art depended to a great extent on scientific investigation, and his famous drawings of *The Anatomy of the Horse* (1766) are based on his own dissections undertaken over a number of years in Lincolnshire. When turning science into art Stubbs imposed a strict sense of pattern, with the forms often placed in front of a low horizon so that they are silhouetted against the sky.

Many of the paintings by Stubbs in the Royal Collection have personal associations with George IV, but this also gives them variety and serves to remind the viewer that Stubbs's oeuvre comprises a wide range of subject matter. This is the case with *Soldiers of the Tenth Light Dragoons*. In addition to being a keen horseman, George IV also had a passionate interest in military matters, especially the history and creation of new regiments and the design of uniforms. He was, in fact, appointed Colonel Commandant of the Tenth (or The Prince of Wales's Own) Regiment of (Light) Dragoons by his father on 29 January 1793 and served as Colonel from 1796 to 1819. The Tenth Light Dragoons were officially designated Hussars after 1805. While the regiment was near Brighton in 1793 George IV visited and sometimes camped with the Tenth Light Dragoons. He celebrated his thirty-first birthday (12 August 1793) with the regiment, partaking of 'a camp dinner' and 'seeing the line fire a *feu de joye*' in his honour. It is possible that the

Soldiers of the Tenth Light Dragoons

1793
Oil on canvas
102.2 × 127 cm
Signed and dated: *Geo: Stubbs p:/1793*

celebration might have been a decisive factor in commissioning this picture from Stubbs.

The painting is remarkable for its directness and detailed observation, but it is not without humour. The accuracy with which the uniforms and accoutrements (note the Prince of Wales's feathers on the saddle, cloth and holster flaps) have been depicted forms a striking contrast with the generalized setting and simplified composition. The interplay between the verticals and horizontals created by the figures is counterbalanced by the undulating landscape, while the sky and the shadows on the ground unite the various parts of the composition. The effect of the figures is not dissimilar to musical notation.

The presentation of the soldiers is severely formal, but the artist's desire to be objective is almost undermined by the characterization of the soldiers with their individual facial features and splayed feet. Although they cannot be identified by name, their ranks are evident. A mounted sergeant with his sword at the carry is on the left; a trumpeter, a sergeant shouldering arms and a private presenting arms stand in a line to the right. The two sergeants and the private are wearing 'tarleton' helmets, named after the light cavalry officer Colonel Sir Banastre Tarleton, who designed and wore this headdress during the American War of Independence. The trumpeter, who had responsibility for relaying orders to the soldiers, has a jacket with reversed colours to make him more conspicuous on the field of battle. The mounted sergeant wears riding boots and spurs, and the others wear short boots as part of their dismounted dress order. Many aspects of the uniform were incorporated from Continental regiments.

FROM WINDSOR CASTLE

REFERENCES: Millar, 1969, No. 1115; *George Stubbs 1724—1806*, The Tate Gallery, London, 1984, No. 136; *The Royal Collection: Paintings from Windsor Castle*, National Museum of Wales, Cardiff, 1990, No. 48; *Carlton House: The Past Glories of George IV's Palace*, The Queen's Gallery, Buckingham Palace, 1991, No. 61.

27

SIR THOMAS LAWRENCE

1769–1830

Sir Walter Scott (1771–1832)

1821–26
Oil on canvas
161.9 × 133.3 cm

The portrait was commissioned by George IV, who had an immense admiration for both the writer and the artist. Scott had an unconcealed appreciation of Lawrence's portraits, and the painter was an avid reader of Scott's novels. The result was the most vivid and successful of the numerous portraits of the writer, who was one of the two most frequently painted private figures of his day – the other being the Duke of Wellington. Lawrence's skill in depicting not just the likeness of Scott but also his character was attested by contemporaries. Scott himself was deeply flattered that the portrait was commissioned personally by the King and that when finished it was hung in the Grand Corridor in Windsor Castle (Fig. 9). On 12 November 1826 he recorded in his *Journal* the amazement he felt as the painter being able to make 'so much out of an old weather-beaten block', and on 14 November he wrote to his cousin, Mrs Scott of Harden, that 'The portrait is a very fine one and makes me think I have been a very illused gentleman on former occasions'.

The painting was begun early in 1821, and at first progress was rapid. Lawrence was able to capture a compelling likeness of the head with little difficulty as this was his particular skill. Delays began to occur, however, over such matters as the pose, costume and the background. There was then a lapse of two years, but both author and painter were anxious to complete the commission, so the portrait was brought to a rapid conclusion in October and November of 1826. Only at this late stage was it decided to include a view of the Eildon Hills in the background on the left. The portrait was exhibited at the Royal Academy in 1827, but Lawrence did not deliver it to George IV until November 1828. Even at this late stage he made yet another small alteration by adding to one of the manuscripts on the table the title *The Fair Maid of Perth*, a book that was only published in 1828.

Lawrence enjoyed painting Scott and gives an interesting account of how he engaged the sitter's interest. The sittings often took place at seven in the morning, and the painter found Scott a difficult proposition. 'I had selected what struck me as his noblest look, but when he was in the chair before me, he talked away on all sorts of subjects in his usual style, so that it cost me great pains to bring him back to solemnity, when I had to attend to any thing beyond the outline of a subordinate feature. I soon found that the surest recipe was to say something that would lead him to recite a bit of poetry. I used to introduce, by hook or by crook, a few lines of Campbell or Byron – he was sure to take up the passage where I left it, or *cap* it by something better – and then – when he was, as Dryden says of one of his heroes – "Made up of three parts fire – so full of Heaven/It sparkled in his eyes" – then was my time – and I made the best use I could of it.'

Born in Edinburgh, Scott was a historical novelist, poet and dramatist. Trained in the law, he was able with the early success of his Scottish ballads and medieval romances in 1812 to buy an estate at Abbotsford in the Borders on the banks of the River Tweed where he built a baronial mansion. The Waverley Novels, published anonymously between 1814 and 1832, are one of the highpoints of nineteenth-century literature. Scott organized the parades, pageantry and receptions for George IV's State Visit to Scotland in 1822. The King was greeted on arrival at Leith by Scott and declared him to be 'The man in Scotland I most wish to see'.

Lawrence was an infant prodigy and succeeded Sir Joshua Reynolds as Principal Painter to George III in 1792. His style, characterized by bravura brushwork, vivid colouring, lush distribution of paint and striking poses was more suited to the reign of George IV. As a portraitist of both men and women, Lawrence rivals Goya and Delacroix. A considerable collector and connoisseur in his day, Lawrence was elected President of the Royal Academy in 1820.

FROM WINDSOR CASTLE

REFERENCES: Millar, 1969, No. 913; F. Russell, *Portraits of Sir Walter Scott*, London, 1987, pp. 12–13, 56–59 and No. 115; *The Royal Collection: Paintings from Windsor Castle*, National Museum of Wales, Cardiff, 1990, No. 34.

28

JACQUES-LAURENT AGASSE

1767–1849

The Nubian Giraffe

1827
Oil on canvas
127.3 × 102 cm
Signed lower right: *J.L.A*

The giraffe is depicted in a special enclosure of the Royal Menagerie that was established in the mid-eighteenth century at Sandpit Gate in Windsor Great Park. The animal is attended by two Arab keepers and most probably by Edward Cross, who wears a top hat and was instructed by George IV to oversee the arrangements for the arrival of the giraffe in England. Cross was a leading importer of exotic animals and at that time ran a popular menagerie known as the Exeter 'Change, located on the Strand in London. He supplied George IV with animals for the Royal Menagerie from 1824 and later founded the Surrey Literary, Scientific and Zoological Institution and Garden in Kennington, which for several years had a greater reputation than the London Zoological Society (the present London Zoo).

The giraffe was one of two calves that in 1826 had been captured on the plains of Sennaar in the Sudan. Having shot the mother, the soldiers strapped the giraffes to the backs of camels and travelled to Cairo, a journey of forty-five days. Mehemet Ali, Pasha of Egypt, decided to offer the smaller calf to George IV and the larger one to Charles X of France. From Cairo the giraffes travelled to Alexandria before being separated. The specimen for George IV was shipped to Malta, where it rested for six months before continuing the voyage to London. It arrived at Waterloo Bridge on the evening of Saturday, 11 August 1827, accompanied by two Arab keepers and two Egyptian cows, which can be seen behind the giraffe in the present picture. From central London the animal was taken to Windsor a few days later. Unfortunately, the giraffe had not travelled well and, much weakened by the journey, had lost the use of its legs. An elaborate pulley was constructed with a sling attached in order to support the giraffe while standing (not shown in the painting), but the animal died towards the end of 1829. The skin was stuffed by Gould and Tomkins and presented by William IV to the London Zoological Society. When the society's museum was dispersed in 1855, the stuffed skin was acquired by Dr Crisp, a zoological pathologist. Its present whereabouts is not known.

The arrival of the giraffe in London was a well-publicized event, and it was painted not only by Agasse but by R. B. Davis, who was later appointed animal painter to William IV. Davis shows the giraffe in a variety of poses but in an oriental setting. There are also several written descriptions of its appearance. The greatest excitement engendered by the arrival of the giraffe, however, was registered by political cartoonists. George IV was at that stage of his life amorously entangled with Lady Conyngham, and caricaturists like William Heath, William Seymour and John Doyle took advantage of the situation. The giraffe seemed in the public's eyes to symbolize yet another example of George IV's extravagance.

Agasse was a painter of Swiss origin born in Geneva. He was one of J. L. David's numerous pupils in Paris (1786–9) and thereafter worked for a short time in Geneva and Lausanne before finally settling in London in 1800. His reputation rests mainly on his sporting pictures, but he also did portraits, views of London and genre scenes that in some respects resemble works by Biedermeier artists. As well as having several aristocratic patrons like Lord Rivers and Lord Heathfield, who may have introduced him to George IV, Agasse also knew Edward Cross and frequently visited the Exeter 'Change.

FROM WINDSOR CASTLE

REFERENCES: Millar, 1969, No. 651; *Jacques-Laurent Agasse 1767–1848*. The Tate Gallery, London, 1988, No. 59; Essen, Kulturstiftung Ruhr, Villa Hugel; *London – World City 1800–1840*, Eng. edition, New Haven and London, 1992, No. 341.

29

FRANS XAVER WINTERHALTER

1805–1873

The First of May

1851

1851
Oil on canvas
106.7 × 129.5 cm
Signed and dated: *F. Winterhalter*
1851

Winterhalter, who was born in the Black Forest in Germany, was the principal portrait painter at the court of Queen Victoria during the first half of her reign. That he was preferred above British painters was the subject of some critical comment. His reputation is based on his work at the leading European courts. He first came to London in 1842 on the recommendation of Louise, Queen of the Belgians, and he continued to work for Queen Victoria at intervals until his death, painting well over a hundred pictures. He was primarily a peripatetic artist of a truly international status and sustained a high level of productivity with the help of studio assistants, amassing a considerable financial fortune. Although Winterhalter held no official appointment, he was nonetheless given important commissions by Queen Victoria, who admired Winterhalter for his ability to obtain a good likeness and for his light, fresh colours. His portraits are indeed sympathetic, occasionally inventive and invariably soundly constructed, but at the same time it has to be acknowledged that they are not always accurately drawn and that the brushwork sometimes veers dangerously from the dexterous to the meretricious.

Winterhalter was frequently commissioned by Queen Victoria to paint subjects of private significance. *The First of May 1851* is one such example and is replete with family allusions. The Queen holds Prince Arthur, Duke of Connaught (1850–1942), who presents a small bunch of lilies of the valley to his godfather, the aged Duke of Wellington, who in turn hands the young prince a casket. Behind these figures, forming the apex of the pyramidal composition, is Prince Albert. He half looks over his shoulder towards the Crystal Palace, visible in the left background. The title of the painting is derived from the fact that both Prince Arthur and the Duke of Wellington were born on 1 May (the Duke of Wellington in 1769 and Prince Arthur in 1850) and that 1 May 1851 was the inauguration date of the Great Exhibition in Hyde Park. The Crystal Palace (the appellation was due to *Punch* magazine) was the central building in the Exhibition, an event that united industry and the arts in a celebration of all aspects of modernity as exemplified by Britain, which at that time was the most advanced industrial nation in the world. Prince Albert played a pivotal role in organizing the exhibition. Both Prince Albert and the Duke of Wellington wear the uniforms of the rank of Field Marshal and the ribands of the Order of the Garter. In a later explanation in a letter to Prince Albert (20 April 1871) Queen Victoria admitted that the purpose was 'to represent an Event, like Rubens – & Paul Veronese did, *periods* of history – *without any exact fact*'. The Queen also records that the Duke of Wellington gave his godson 'a Cup and model of my throne – Papa suggested something more *picturesque* than the *cup* shd be put into the duke's hand wh wd equally *tell* the story and so a pretty box *now* on my Table which dear Papa gave me, was taken & painted in!' She then remarks, 'it only shows how wrong in fact it is not to paint things as they really are'.

Formulating an appropriate composition apparently caused Winterhalter some difficulty. On 21 May 1851 Queen Victoria wrote in her journal that the artist 'did not seem to know how to carry it out, so dear Albert with his wonderful knowledge & taste, gave Winterhalter the idea, which is now to be carried out'. The 'idea' was to conceive of the composition as an Adoration of the Magi as suggested by the iconography. Indeed, the finished picture is to a certain extent reminiscent of paintings of that subject by sixteenth-century Italian artists, such as Paolo Veronese.

Prince Arthur was Queen Victoria's third son. As befitted a godson of the Duke of Wellington, he pursued an active military career, distinguishing himself during the Egyptian campaign of 1882, and was promoted to the rank of Field Marshal in 1902. He subsequently became Governor-General of Canada (1911) before retiring from public life in 1928.

FROM WINDSOR CASTLE
REFERENCES: Millar, 1992, No. 827.

30

ELIZABETH THOMPSON, LADY BUTLER

1846–1933

The Roll Call: Calling the Roll after an Engagement, Crimea

1874
Oil on canvas
927 × 183.8 cm
Signed and dated lower left: *Eliz Thompson/1874* below a cypher
C+

The Roll Call was one of the most popular paintings ever exhibited in Britain during the nineteenth century. When it was shown at the Royal Academy in the early summer of 1874 the artist received universal acclaim. The demand to see it was such that a policeman was posted in front of the picture to control the crowds, a precaution taken only on two previous occasions, namely for Sir David Wilkie's *Chelsea Pensioners receiving the London Gazette Extraordinary of Thursday June 22, 1815, announcing the Battle of Waterloo* (1822) and W. P. Frith's *Derby Day* (1858). In a speech at the Royal Academy Dinner (2 May 1874), the Prince of Wales (the future Edward VII) referred to *The Roll Call* as 'deserving of the highest admiration'. Subsequently, the painting went on tour and was seen in Newcastle-upon-Tyne, Leeds, Birmingham, Liverpool and Oxford. Special *carte de visite* photographs of the artist were issued, and the picture's arrival was heralded in each city by men wearing sandwich-boards announcing, '*The Roll Call* is coming'. Even in this century the success of the painting was still being acknowledged with a re-enactment of the composition in 1909 by the Grenadier Guards at the Aldershot Military Tattoo.

The Roll Call was painted when the artist was only twenty-eight and immediately established Lady Butler as the foremost painter of military scenes in Britain. It portrays the aftermath of battle. The remnants of a battalion of Grenadier Guards, many of whom are wounded or exhausted, are answering the roll being read out by a sergeant before a mounted officer who was later identified as Captain George Higginson. The desolate landscape, snow streaked with blood and the circling birds of prey create a sombre scene. The title refers to the Crimean War (1854–60), in which Britain and France fought to protect Turkey from invasion by Russia, but the subject has often been associated specifically with the Battle of Inkerman (5 November 1854). Lady Butler, however, who went on to paint other scenes from the Crimean War (*Balaclava* (1876), Manchester City Art Galleries, and *The Return from Inkerman*, (1877), Hull, Ferens Art Gallery), seems to have intended the image to be a general statement about the Crimean War emphasizing the horrors and realism of battle as experienced by ordinary soldiers. Indeed, it is the pathos of war and not the more romantic conception of heroism that is the theme of *The Roll Call*.

The Crimean War had been widely reported, notably in *The Illustrated London News*, and the deficiencies of the senior ranks in the British Army exposed. *The Roll Call*, therefore, has to be seen in the context of the military reforms begun in 1870. The public attention paid to the Crimean War also accounts for Lady Butler's meticulous preparations for the picture. She took particular care over such details as the uniforms, consulted soldiers who had been in the Crimea, searched for suitable models and made numerous oil studies and watercolours before transferring them to canvas. The painting was innovative not only in its depiction of war but in its treatment. The flat relief-like composition, subdued colour, emphasis on the foreground, emotional detachment and the resort to anecdote had not been used in British battle painting before, and such devices reveal the influence of French painters like Edouard Détaille, Jean-Louis-Ernest Meissonier and Alfonse de Neuville, whose work Lady Butler acknowledged. The Guards Memorial in Waterloo Place, London, sculpted by John Bell (1860) may also have inspired the artist.

The Roll Call had in fact been commissioned by the industrialist Charles Galloway, but after some persuasion he agreed in May 1874 to cede it to Queen Victoria, who had taken a special interest in the Crimean War and had expressed concern about the plight of ordinary soldiers.

FROM ST JAMES'S PALACE
REFERENCES: Millar, 1992, No. 185; Lloyd, 1991, No. 77.

GENEALOGICAL TREE OF ROYAL COLLECTORS

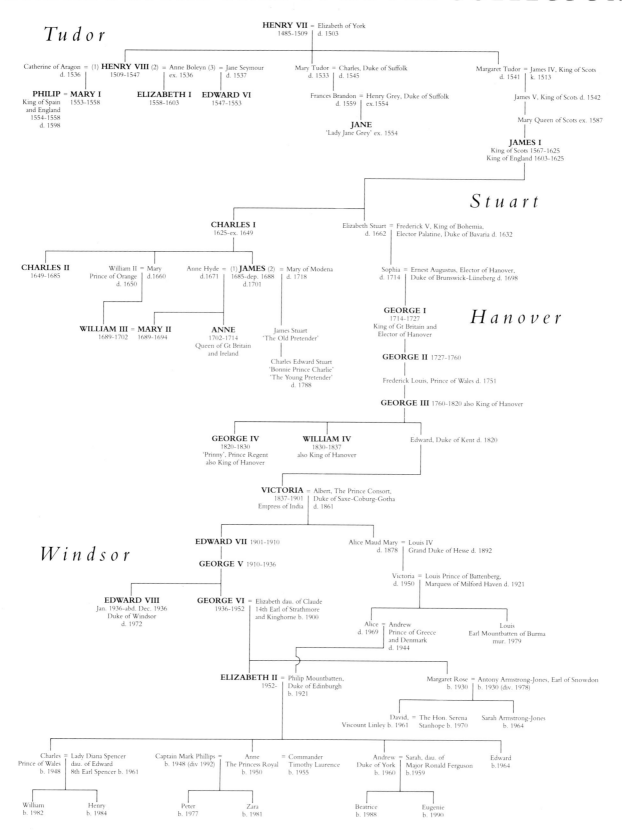

Tudor

HENRY VII = Elizabeth of York
1485-1509   d. 1503

Catherine of Aragon = (1) **HENRY VIII** (2) = Anne Boleyn (3) = Jane Seymour
d. 1536   1509-1547   ex. 1536   d. 1537

Mary Tudor = Charles, Duke of Suffolk
d. 1533   d. 1545

Margaret Tudor = James IV, King of Scots
d. 1541   k. 1513

PHILIP = **MARY I**
King of Spain   1553-1558
and England
1554-1558
d. 1598

ELIZABETH I
1558-1603

EDWARD VI
1547-1553

Frances Brandon = Henry Grey, Duke of Suffolk
d. 1559   ex.1554

James V, King of Scots d. 1542

JANE
'Lady Jane Grey' ex. 1554

Mary Queen of Scots ex. 1587

JAMES I
King of Scots 1567-1625
King of England 1603-1625

Stuart

CHARLES I
1625-ex. 1649

Elizabeth Stuart = Frederick V, King of Bohemia,
d. 1662   Elector Palatine, Duke of Bavaria d. 1632

CHARLES II
1649-1685

William II = Mary
Prince of Orange   d.1660
d. 1650

Anne Hyde = (1) **JAMES** (2) = Mary of Modena
d.1671   1685-dep. 1688   d. 1718
d.1701

Sophia = Ernest Augustus, Elector of Hanover,
d. 1714   Duke of Brunswick-Lüneberg d. 1698

WILLIAM III = **MARY II**
1689-1702   1689-1694

ANNE
1702-1714
Queen of Gt Britain
and Ireland

James Stuart
'The Old Pretender'

GEORGE I
1714-1727
King of Gt Britain and
Elector of Hanover

Hanover

Charles Edward Stuart
'Bonnie Prince Charlie'
'The Young Pretender'
d. 1788

GEORGE II 1727-1760

Frederick Louis, Prince of Wales d. 1751

GEORGE III 1760-1820 also King of Hanover

GEORGE IV
1820-1830
'Prinny', Prince Regent
also King of Hanover

WILLIAM IV
1830-1837
also King of Hanover

Edward, Duke of Kent d. 1820

VICTORIA = Albert, The Prince Consort,
1837-1901   Duke of Saxe-Coburg-Gotha
Empress of India   d. 1861

EDWARD VII 1901-1910

Alice Maud Mary = Louis IV
d. 1878   Grand Duke of Hesse d. 1892

Windsor

GEORGE V 1910-1936

Victoria = Louis Prince of Battenberg,
d. 1950   Marquess of Milford Haven d. 1921

EDWARD VIII
Jan. 1936-abd. Dec. 1936
Duke of Windsor
d. 1972

GEORGE VI = Elizabeth dau. of Claude
1936-1952   14th Earl of Strathmore
and Kinghorne b. 1900

Alice = Andrew
d. 1969   Prince of Greece
and Denmark
d. 1944

Louis
Earl Mountbatten of Burma
mur. 1979

ELIZABETH II = Philip Mountbatten,
1952-   Duke of Edinburgh
b. 1921

Margaret Rose = Antony Armstrong-Jones, Earl of Snowdon
b. 1930   b. 1930 (div. 1978)

David, = The Hon. Serena
Viscount Linley b. 1961   Stanhope b. 1970

Sarah Armstrong-Jones
b. 1964

Charles = Lady Diana Spencer
Prince of Wales   dau. of Edward
b. 1948   8th Earl Spencer b. 1961

Captain Mark Phillips =
b. 1948 (div 1992)

Anne
The Princess Royal
b. 1950

= Commander
Timothy Laurence
b. 1955

Andrew = Sarah, dau. of
Duke of York   Major Ronald Ferguson
b. 1960   b.1959

Edward
b.1964

William
b. 1982

Henry
b. 1984

Peter
b. 1977

Zara
b. 1981

Beatrice
b. 1988

Eugenie
b. 1990

FURTHER READING

GENERAL

C. Lloyd (with an essay by Sir Oliver Millar), *The Queen's Pictures: Royal Collectors through the Centuries*, London, 1991.

C. Lloyd, *The Royal Collection: A Thematic Exploration of the Paintings in the Collection of Her Majesty The Queen*, London, 1992.

O. Millar, *The Queen's Pictures*, London, 1977.

J. H. Plumb and H. Wheldon, *Royal Heritage: The Story of Britain's Royal Builders and Collectors*, London, 1977.

J. H. Plumb and H. Wheldon, *Royal Heritage: The Reign of Elizabeth II*, London, 1981.

CATALOGUES

L. Campbell, *The Early Flemish Pictures in the Collection of Her Majesty The Queen*, Cambridge University Press, 1985.

M. Levey, *The Later Italian Pictures in the Collection of Her Majesty The Queen*, 2nd edition, Cambridge University Press, 1991.

A. Martindale, *The Triumphs of Caesar by Andrea Mantegna in the Collection of Her Majesty The Queen at Hampton Court*, London, 1979.

O. Millar, *The Tudor, Stuart, and Early Georgian Pictures in the Collection of Her Majesty The Queen*, London, 1963.

O. Millar, *The Later Georgian Pictures in the Collection of Her Majesty The Queen*, London, 1969.

O. Millar, *The Victorian Pictures in the Collection of Her Majesty The Queen*, Cambridge University Press, 1992.

J. Shearman, *Raphael's Cartoons in the Collection of Her Majesty The Queen*, London, 1972.

J. Shearman, *The Early Italian Pictures in the Collection of Her Majesty The Queen*, Cambridge University Press, 1983.

C. White, *The Dutch Pictures in the Collection of Her Majesty The Queen*, Cambridge University Press, 1982.

R. Walker, *Miniatures in the Collection of Her Majesty The Queen: The Eighteenth and Early Nineteenth Centuries*, Cambridge University Press, 1992.

OTHER TITLES

J. Roberts, *Royal Artists from Mary Queen of Scots to the Present Day*, London, 1987.

The Late King's Goods: Collections, Possessions and Patronage of Charles I in the Light of the Commonwealth Sale Inventories, ed. A. MacGregor, London and Oxford, 1989.

Carlton House: The Past Glories of George IV's Palace, The Queen's Gallery, Buckingham Palace, 1991.

A King's Purchase: King George III and the Collection of Consul Smith, The Queen's Gallery, Buckingham Palace, 1992.

INDEX

Numbers in **bold** refer to the pages of catalogue entries; numbers in *italics* refer to pages with figure numbers of comparative illustrations.

Agasse, Jacques-Laurent, *The Nubian Giraffe*, **88–9**
Albert, Prince, 14, 21–2, 23, 26, 27, 30, 90
Alexandra, Queen, 26
Allori, Cristofano, *Judith with the Head of Holofernes*, **40–1**
Amelia, Princess, **82–3**
Angeli, Heinrich von, 21, 27
Anne of Denmark, Queen, 16, 38
Arthur, Prince, Duke of Connaught, 27, **90–1**
Augusta, Princess of Wales, **68–9**

Balmoral Castle, 14, 22, 30, 31
Bassano, Jacopo dal Ponte, *The Adoration of the Shepherds*, **34–5**
Beechey, Sir William, 20, 29, 82
Brueghel the Elder, Jan, 18–19, 58
Buckingham Palace (formerly Buckingham House), 14, 19, 20, 22, 23, 26, 27, 31, *32*, 44, 48, 50, 58, 60, 62, 64, 72, 76, 78
Butler, Lady Elizabeth Thompson, 21; *The Roll Call*, 30, **92–3**

Canaletto, *Venice: the Grand Canal with S. Maria della Salute . . .*, **70–1**
Caravaggio, 16, 17, 40, 42, 46, 48, 54
Carlton House, 20, 26, 31, 32, *32*, 48, 50, 58
Carracci, Annibale, 17; *Head of a Man in Profile*, **36–7**
Charles I, King, 14, *15*, 15–18, 20, 23, 25, 26, 31, 32, 38, 40, 42, 46, 52, 54
Charles II, King, 25, 27, 29, 66, 72
Charlotte, Queen, *19*, 19–20, 26, 27, 80, 82
Claude, Gellée *called* Le Lorrain, *Harbour Scene at Sunset*, **56–7**
Copley, John Singleton, *The Three Youngest Daughters of George III*, 27, **82–3**
Cromwell, Oliver, 18, 27
Cuff, John, **80–1**
Cuyp, Aelbert, 20; *An Evening Landscape with Figures and Sheep*, **60–1**

Dürer, Albrecht, 17, 34
Dyce, William, 22

Edward III, King, 27, 28, 29
Edward VI, King, 24

Edward VII, King, 26, 92
Elizabeth I, Queen, 24, *25*, 38
Elizabeth, Queen Mother, 26
Elizabeth of York, Queen, *24*
Elizabeth, Princess, 82

Fildes, Sir Luke, 26
Francis I, King of France, 27
Frederick, Duke of York, 26
Frederick, Prince of Wales, 14, 18–19, 31, 36, 44, 52, 56, **68–9**, **72–3**
Frogmore House, 14, 82

Gainsborough, Thomas, 20, 26, 27, 52, 82, 90; *James Quin*, **78–9**
Garrick, David, **74–5**, 78, 80
Gentileschi, Artemisia, *Self-Portrait as the Allegory of Painting*, **46–7**
George II, King, 68, 72
George III, King, 14, 19, 23, 25–6, 27, 29, 31, 36, 44, **68–9**, 70, 78, 80, 82
George IV, King, 14, 18, *18*, 20–1, 23, 26, 27, 29, 30, 31, 48, 50, 58, 60, 74, 76, 84, 86, 88
George V, King, 21, 26
George VI, King, 26
Greenwich, Queen's House, 46
Greuze, Jean-Baptiste, *Silence!*, **76–7**

Hals, Frans, 64; *Portrait of a Man*, **44–5**
Hampton Court Palace, 18, 23, 29, 31, 34, 36, 40, 42, 46, 54
Hayter, George, 21, 24–5, 29
Henrietta Maria, Queen, 46, 52, 54
Henry V, King, 24
Henry VII, King, *24*
Henry VIII, King, 14, 23–4, *24*, 27
Henry, Prince of Wales, 14, 16, 30, **38–9**
Hogarth, William, 78; *David Garrick with his wife Eva-Maria Veigel*, **74–5**
Holbein the Younger, Hans, 17, 23, *24*
Holmes, Bridget, **66–7**
Holyroodhouse, Palace of, 14
Hooch, Pieter de, *A Courtyard in Delft at Evening: A Woman Spinning*, **62–3**
Hudson, Thomas, 19, 66, 78
Hyde, Lady Anne, 29

James I, King (James VI of Scotland), 16, 18, 25, 38
James II, King, 29

Kelly, Sir Gerald, 26
Kensington Palace, 14, 31
Kew Palace, 14

Kneller, Sir Godfrey, 29, 66

Landseer, Sir Edwin, 21, 27, 30–1; *Eos*, 30, *30*; *Windsor Castle in Modern Times*, 26
Lawrence, Sir Thomas, 20, 23, 26, 29, 82, 90; *George V*, 18; *Sir Walter Scott*, **86–7**
Leemput, Remigius van, *Henry VII and Elizabeth of York, Henry VIII and Jane Seymour* (after Holbein), 23, *24*
Lely, Sir Peter, 29, 42, 52, 66
Le Nain, Louis, *The Young Card-Players*, **48–9**
Leonardo da Vinci, 16, 17
Louis XIII, King, 54
Loutherbourg, P. J. de, 21

Mantegna, Andrea, 17; *The Triumphs of Caesar*, 18
Mary II, Queen, 29, 31, 66
Mary, Princess, **82–3**
The Monogrammist HE, *Elizabeth I and the Three Goddesses*, 24, *25*
Mytens, Daniel, 25

Nash, Joseph, *Windsor Castle: The Corridor, South*, 32, *32*
Nickolls, Joseph, *St James's Park and The Mall*, **72–3**

Oatlands Palace, 16, 54
Osborne House, 14, 22, 27, 31

Park Place, 68
Passavant, J. D., 31
Peake the Elder, Robert, *Henry, Prince of Wales, in the Hunting-Field*, 30, **38–9**
Philip II, King of Spain, 16
Philip IV, King of Spain, 16, 18
Pyne, William Henry, 31–2, 58

Quin, James, **78–9**

Ramsay, Allan, 23, 25–6, 90
Raphael, 16, 17, 18
Raphael Cartoons, 18
Rembrandt van Rijn, 20, 44, 60; *Christ and the Magdalen at the Tomb*, 20; *Portrait of the Artist's Mother*, 18; '*The Shipbuilder and his Wife*', **50–1**, 74
Reynolds, Sir Joshua, 20, 28, 52, 66, 82, 86
Rijcksen, Jan, **50–1**
Riley, John, *Bridget Holmes*, **66–7**
Robert, David, 21, 30
Royal Pavilion, Brighton, 20, 26

Rubens, Sir Peter Paul, 16, 17, 18, 20, 22, 52; *Landscape with St George*, 20; *Self-Portrait*, 46

St James's Palace, 14, 21, 38, 68, 72, 92
Sandringham House, 14
Scott, Sir Walter, **86–7**
Sophia, Princess, **82–3**
Steen, Jan, 20; *Interior of a Tavern with Card Players and a Violin Player*, **64–5**
Streeter, Robert, 27
Stubbs, George, 20, 27, 30; *The Anatomy of a Horse*, 84; *Soldiers of the Tenth Light Dragoons*, 29, **84–5**

Teniers the Younger, David, 19, 20; *Peasants dancing outside an Inn*, **58–9**
Ter Brugghen, Hendrick, *A Laughing Bravo with a Bass Viol and a Glass*, **42–3**
Titian, 16, 17, 34, 54
Turner, J. M. W., 15, 56; *The Battle of Trafalgar*, 21
Tuxen, Laurits, 21, 29

Van Dyck, Sir Anthony, 16, 17–18, 23, 25, 26, 66, 78, 82, 90; *Charles I*, *15*; *Cupid and Psyche*, 17, 52; *Portrait of a Woman*, **52–3**
Van Somer, Paul, 25
Victoria, Queen, 14, 21–3, 24–5, 26, 27, 29–31, 78, **90–1**, 92
Victoria, Princess, 26
Vouet, Simon, *Diana*, **54–5**

West, Benjamin, 27–9, 82; *The Death of Wolfe*, 27–8, *28*
Whitehall Palace, 14, 23, 31
Wild, Charles, *The Blue Velvet Room: Carlton House*, *32*
Wilkie, Sir David, 21, 29, 92
William III of Orange, King, 29, 31, 64, 66
William IV, King, 23, 26, 29, 88
Windsor Castle, 14, 19, 20, 23, 26, 28–9, 31, 32, *32*, 38, 52, 56, 66, 68, 70, 74, 80, 82, 84, 86, 88, 90
Winterhalter, Frans Xaver, 21, 27, 30; *The First of May 1851*, **90–1**
Wootton, John, 19, 30; *A View of Henley-on-Thames from the East*, **68–9**

Zoffany, Johann, 26, 27, 82; *John Cuff*, **80–1**; *Queen Charlotte at her Dressing Table*, 19, 19–20, 26